A GIFT FOR:

_____

FROM:

_____

God has brought me laughter.
Genesis 21:6

What's That Funny Look on Your Faith?
Copyright © 2006 by Cuyler Black
ISBN-10: 0-310-81397-2
ISBN-13: 978-0-310-81397-2

Requests for information should be addressed to:
Inspirio, the gift group of Zondervan
Grand Rapids, Michigan 49530
www.inspiriogifts.com

Product Manager: Tom Dean
Design Manager: Michael J. Williams
Production Management: Matt Nolan
Design: Michael J. Williams

Printed in China
06 07 08 / 5 4 3 2 1

AN **Inherit the mirth** CARTOON COLLECTION BY CUYLER BLACK

WHAT'S THAT FUNNY LOOK ON YOUR FAITH?

inspirio™

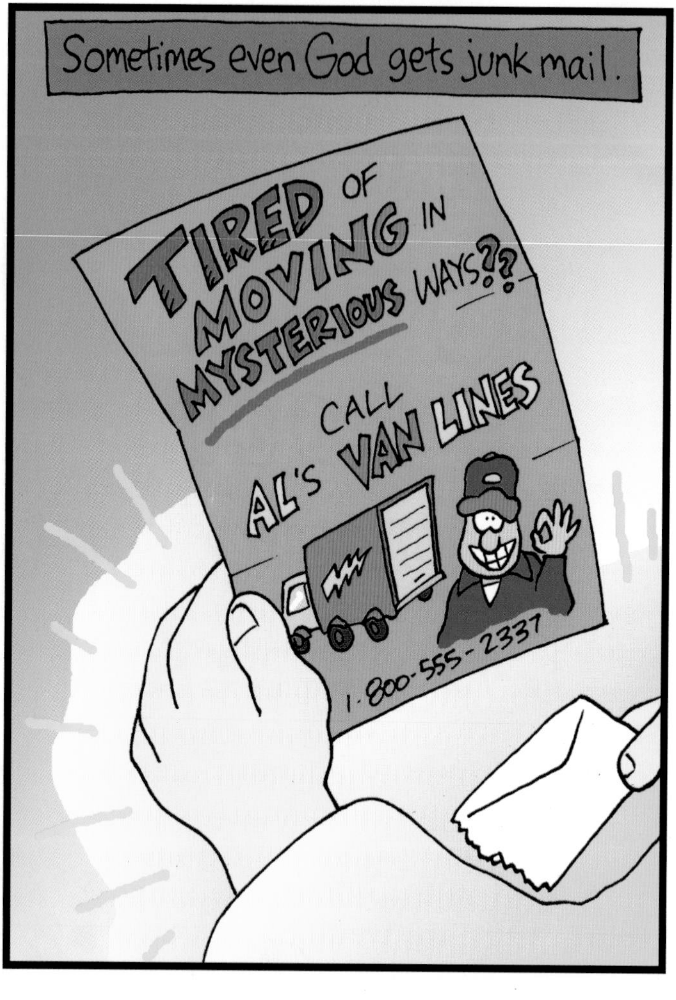
Sometimes even God gets junk mail.
TIRED OF MOVING IN MYSTERIOUS WAYS??
CALL AL'S VAN LINES
1-800-555-2337

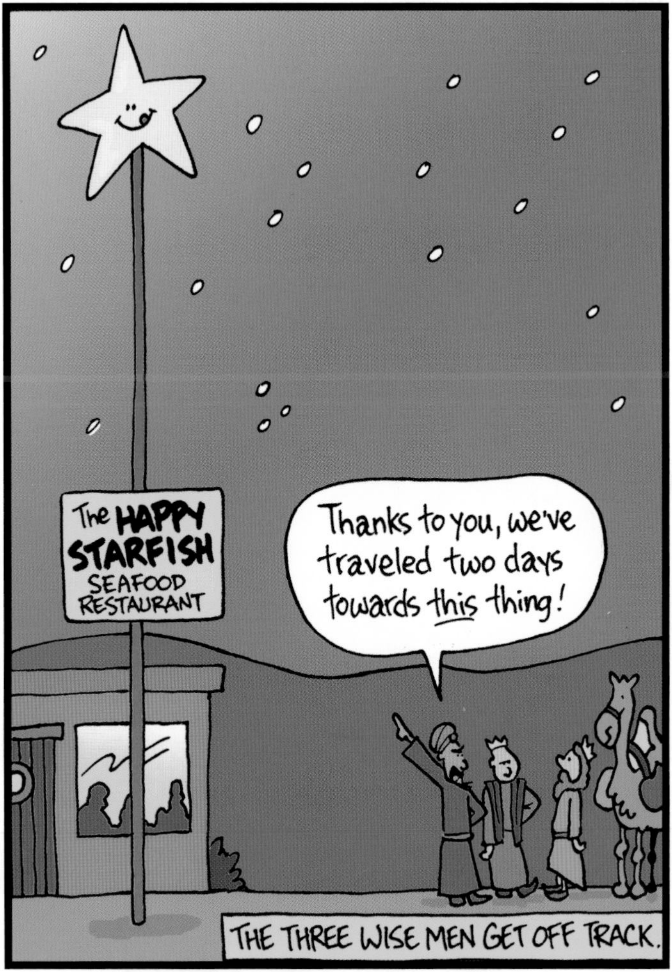
The HAPPY STARFISH SEAFOOD RESTAURANT
Thanks to you, we've traveled two days towards this thing!
THE THREE WISE MEN GET OFF TRACK.

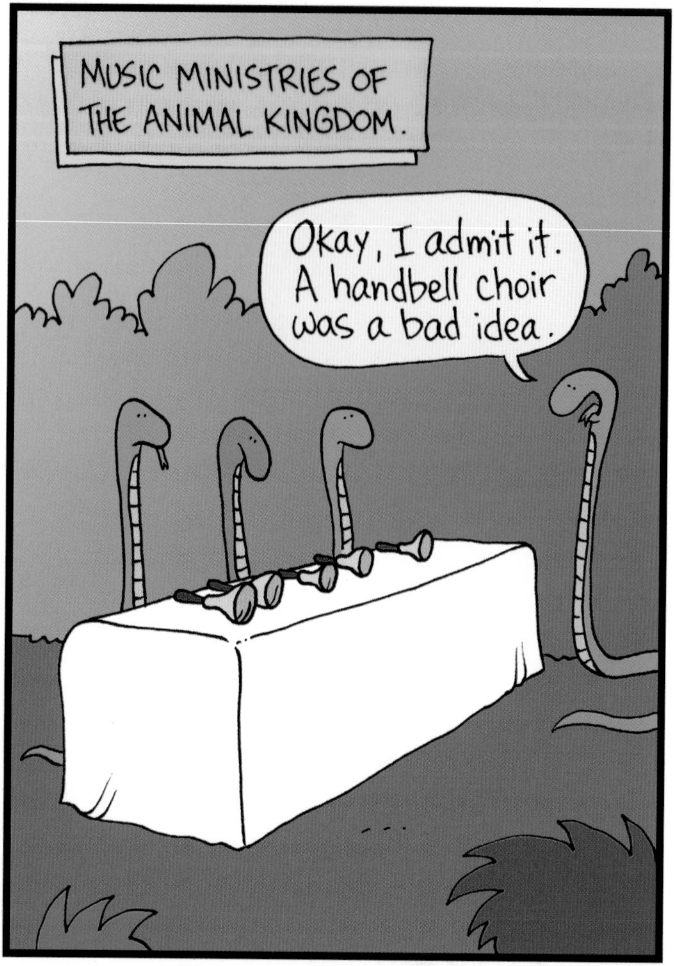
MUSIC MINISTRIES OF THE ANIMAL KINGDOM.
Okay, I admit it. A handbell choir was a bad idea.

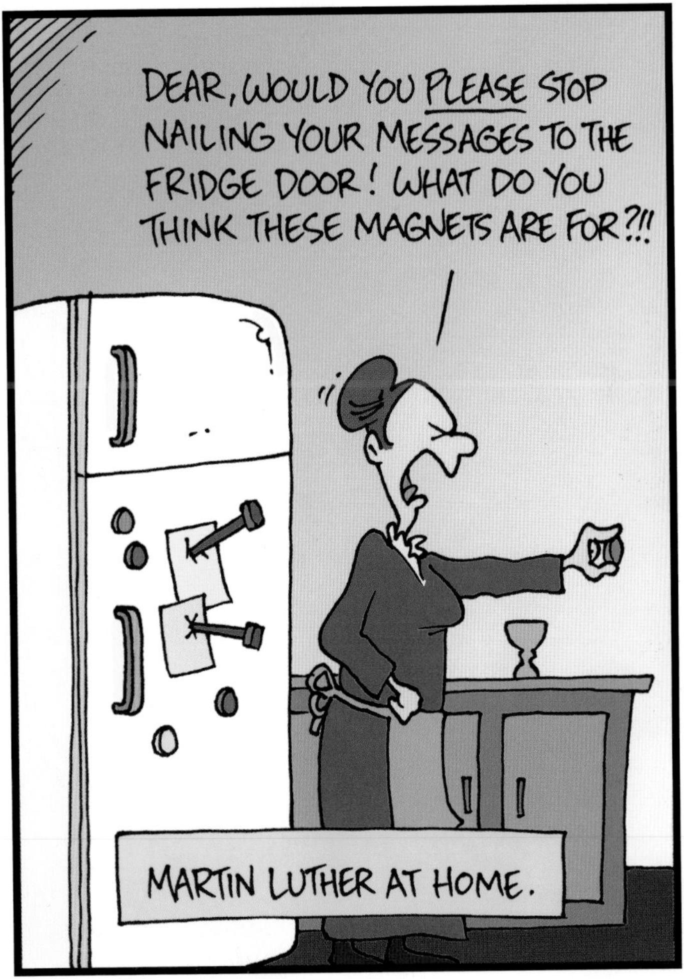
DEAR, WOULD YOU PLEASE STOP NAILING YOUR MESSAGES TO THE FRIDGE DOOR! WHAT DO YOU THINK THESE MAGNETS ARE FOR?!!
MARTIN LUTHER AT HOME.

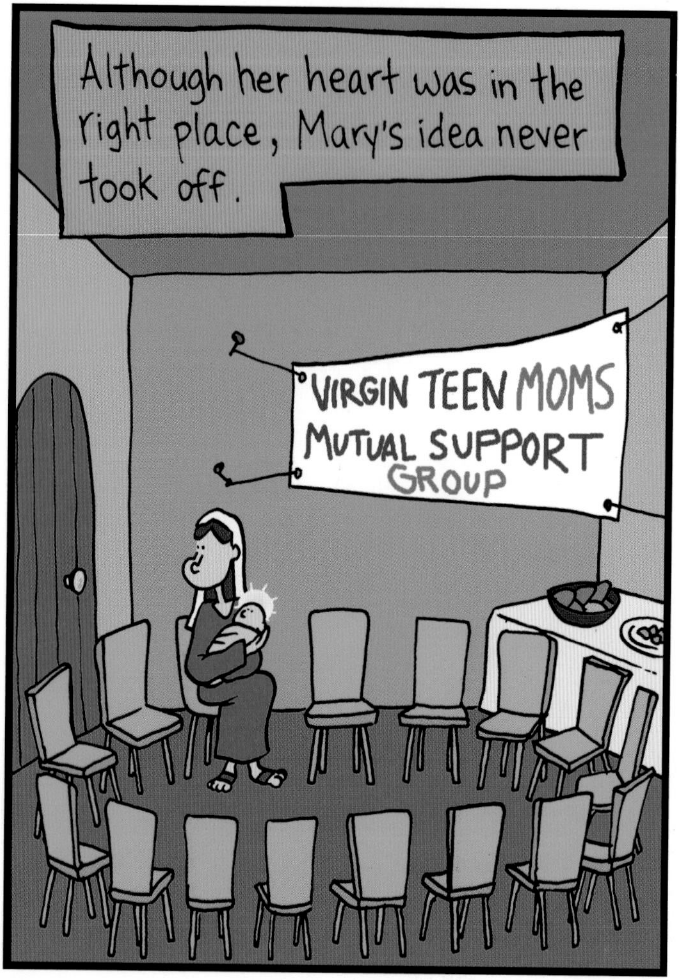
Although her heart was in the right place, Mary's idea never took off.
VIRGIN TEEN MOMS
MUTUAL SUPPORT
GROUP

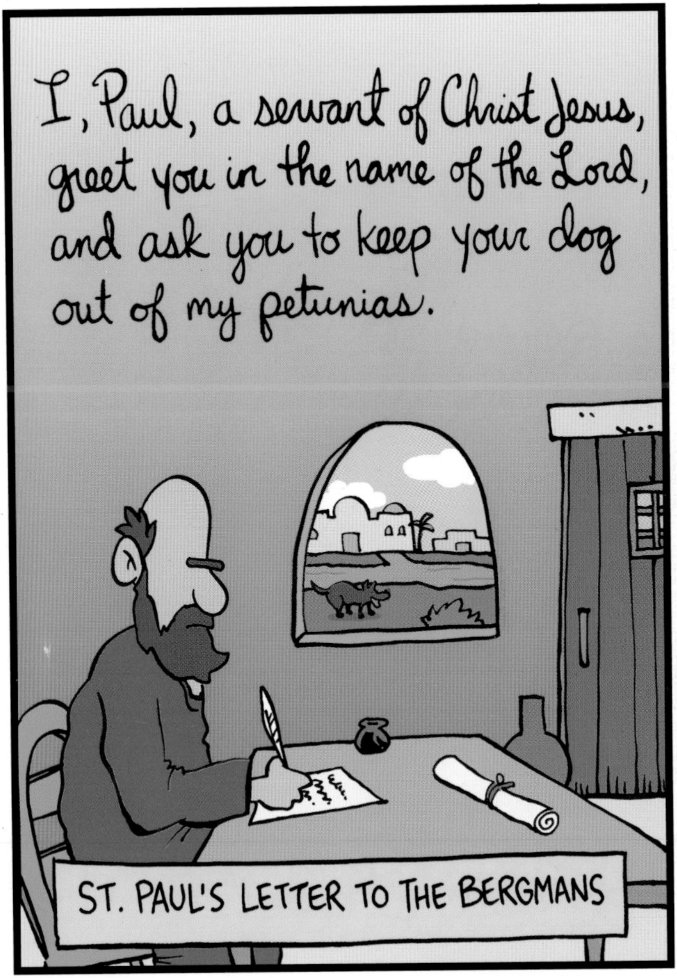
I, Paul, a servant of Christ Jesus, greet you in the name of the Lord, and ask you to keep your dog out of my petunias.
ST. PAUL'S LETTER TO THE BERGMANS

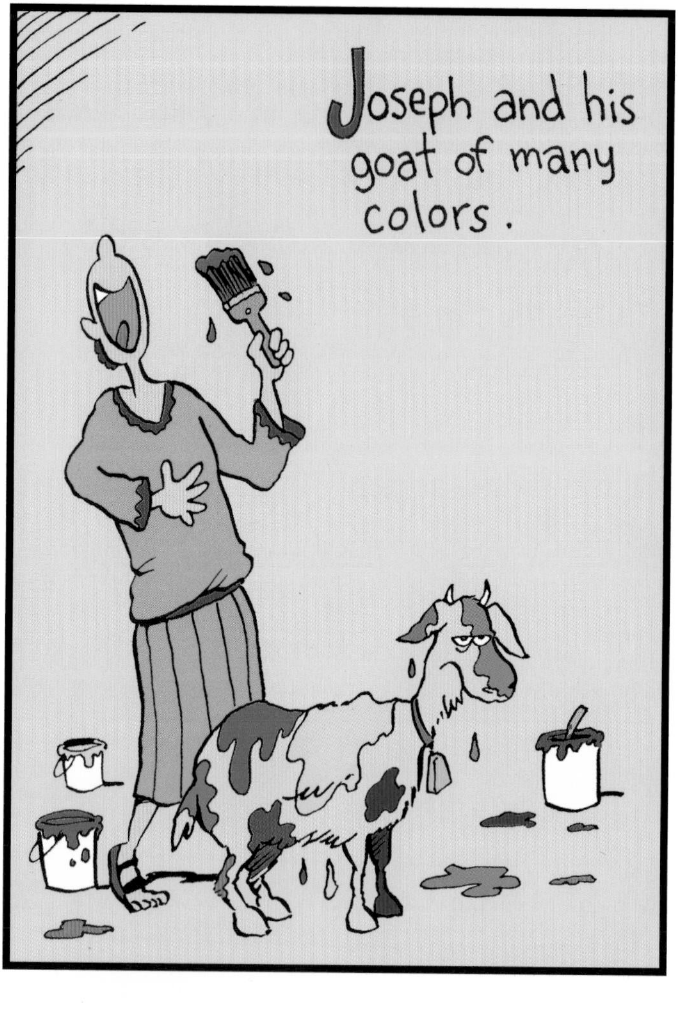
Joseph and his goat of many colors.

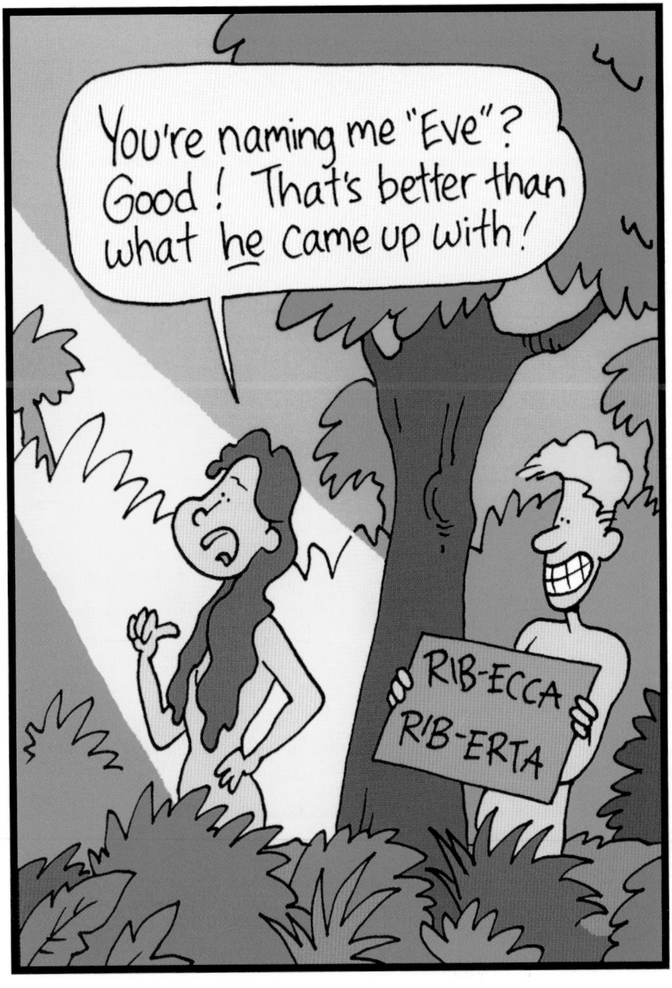
You're naming me "Eve"? Good! That's better than what he came up with!
RIB-ECCA
RIB-ERTA

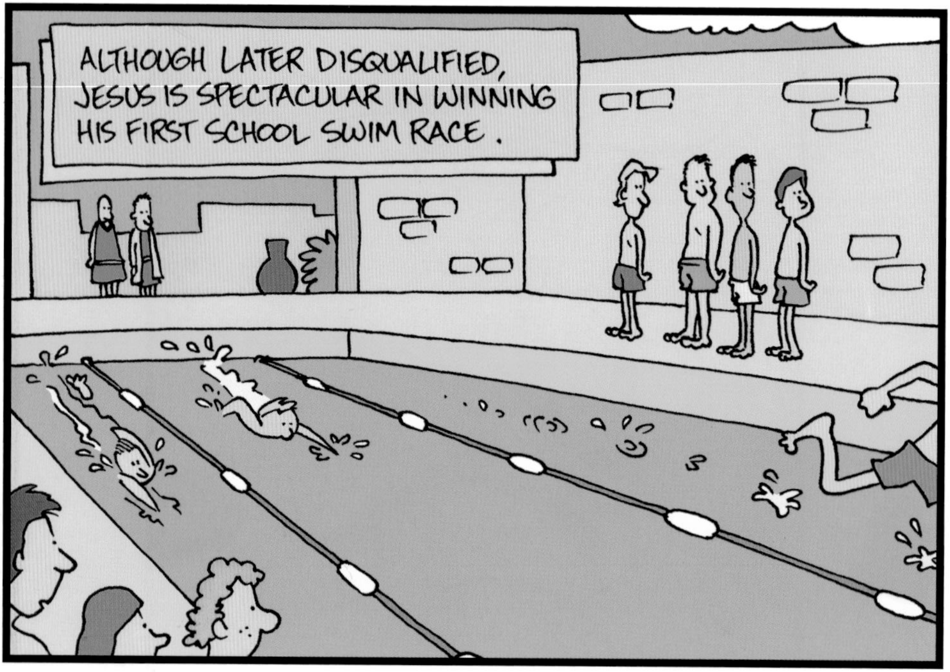
ALTHOUGH LATER DISQUALIFIED, JESUS IS SPECTACULAR IN WINNING HIS FIRST SCHOOL SWIM RACE.

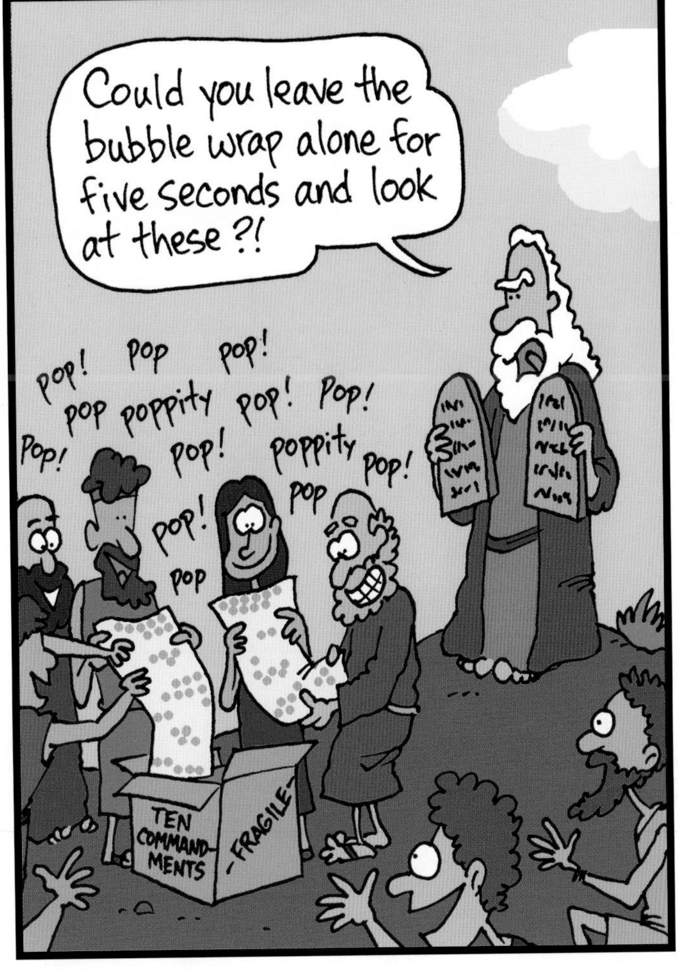
Could you leave the bubble wrap alone for five seconds and look at these?!
pop! pop pop!
pop poppity pop! Pop!
Pop! pop! poppity pop!
pop
pop!
pop
TEN COMMAND-MENTS
-FRAGILE-

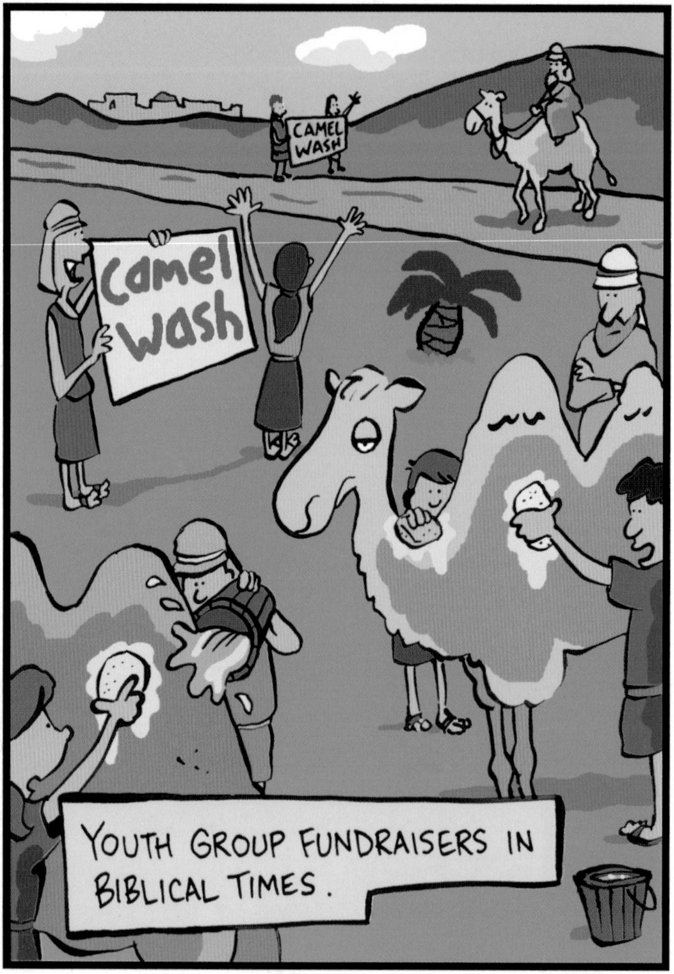
CAMEL WASH
Camel Wash
YOUTH GROUP FUNDRAISERS IN BIBLICAL TIMES.

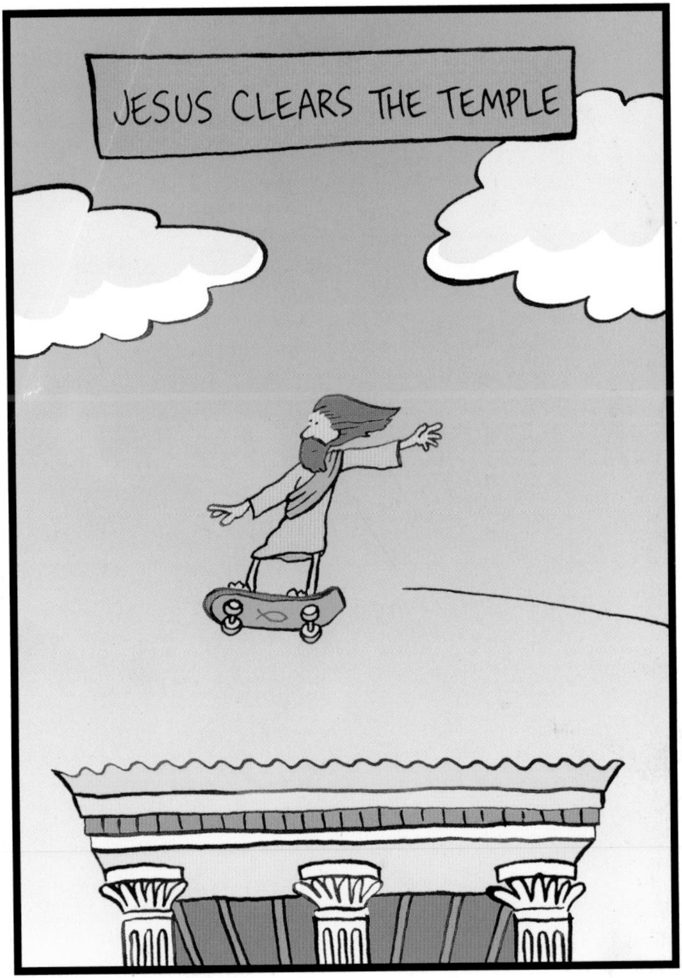
JESUS CLEARS THE TEMPLE

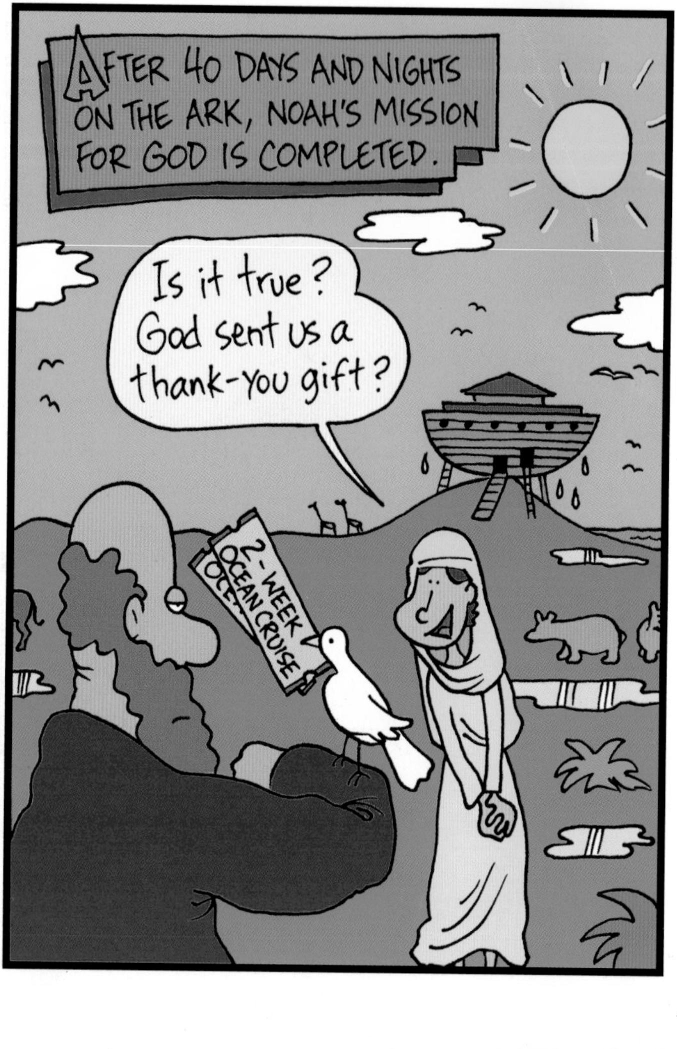
AFTER 40 DAYS AND NIGHTS ON THE ARK, NOAH'S MISSION FOR GOD IS COMPLETED.
Is it true? God sent us a thank-you gift?
2-WEEK OCEAN CRUISE

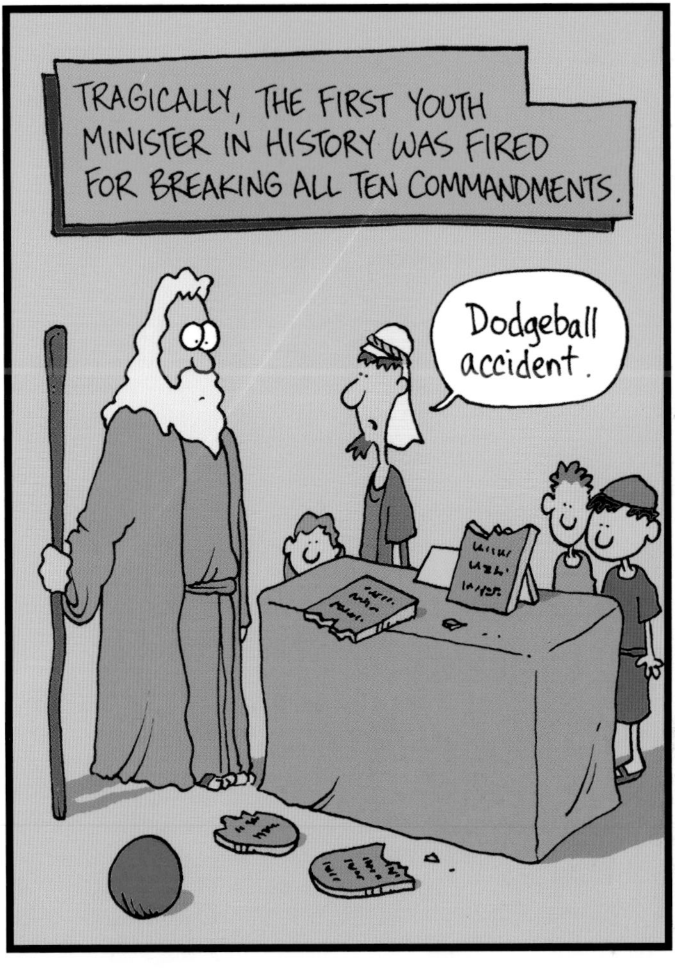
TRAGICALLY, THE FIRST YOUTH MINISTER IN HISTORY WAS FIRED FOR BREAKING ALL TEN COMMANDMENTS.
Dodgeball accident.

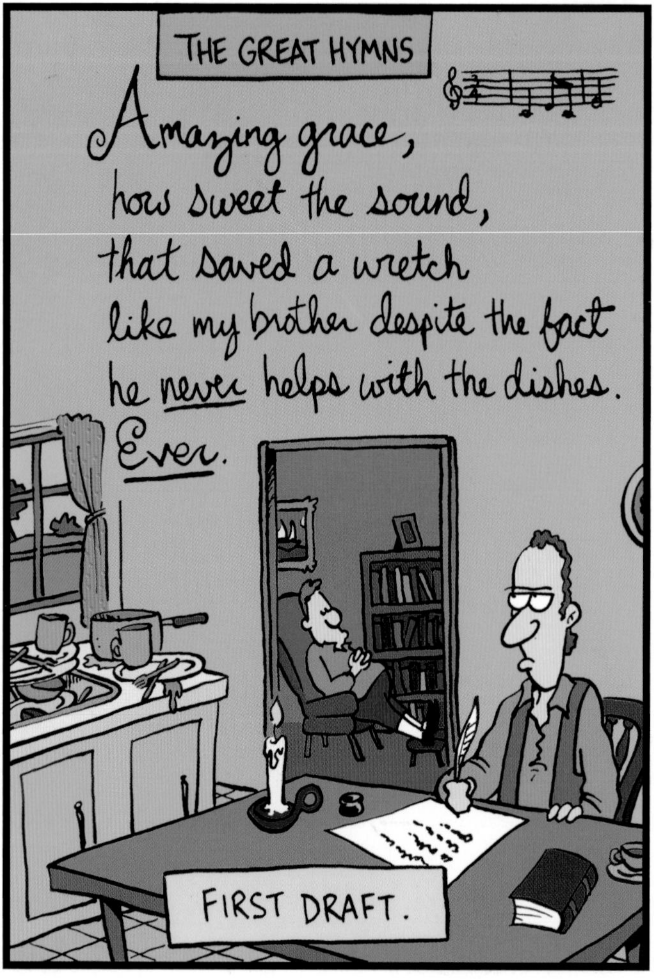
THE GREAT HYMNS
Amazing grace,
how sweet the sound,
that saved a wretch
like my brother despite the fact
he never helps with the dishes.
Ever.
FIRST DRAFT.

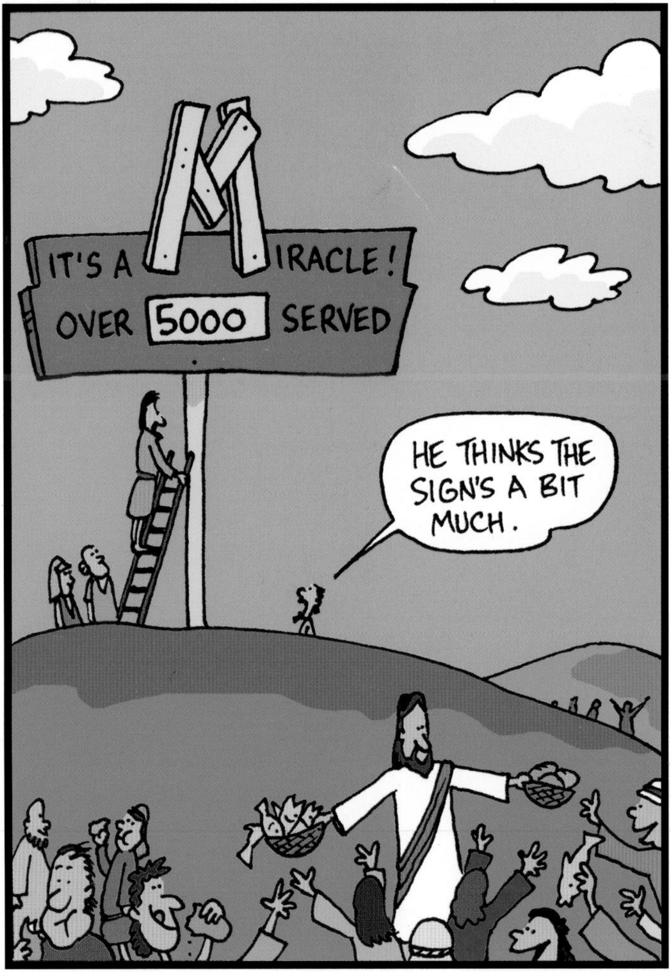
IT'S A MIRACLE!
OVER 5000 SERVED
HE THINKS THE SIGN'S A BIT MUCH.

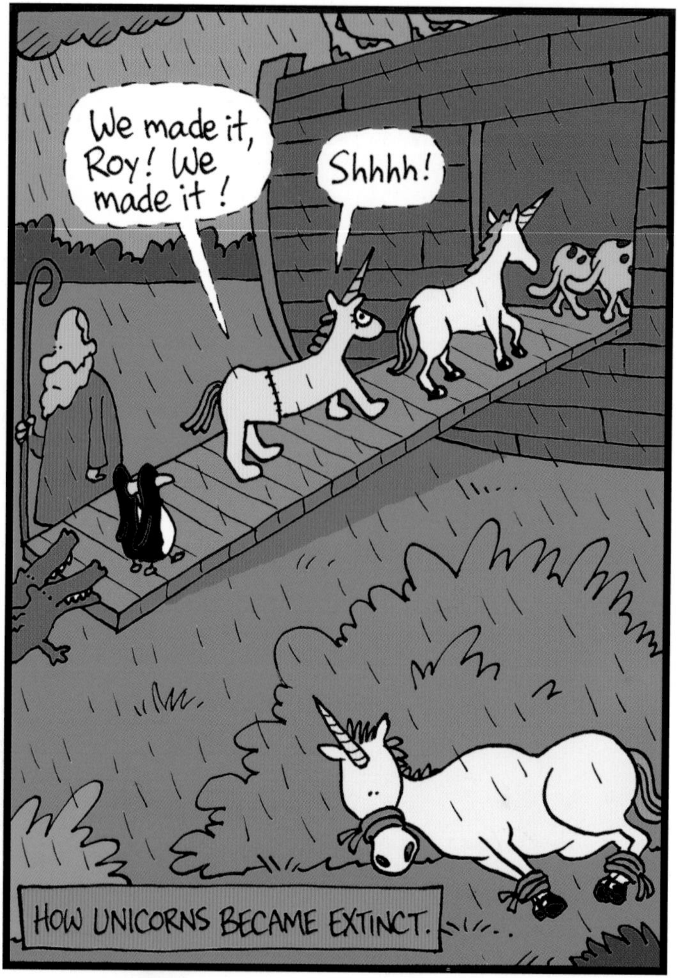
We made it, Roy! We made it!
Shhhh!
HOW UNICORNS BECAME EXTINCT.

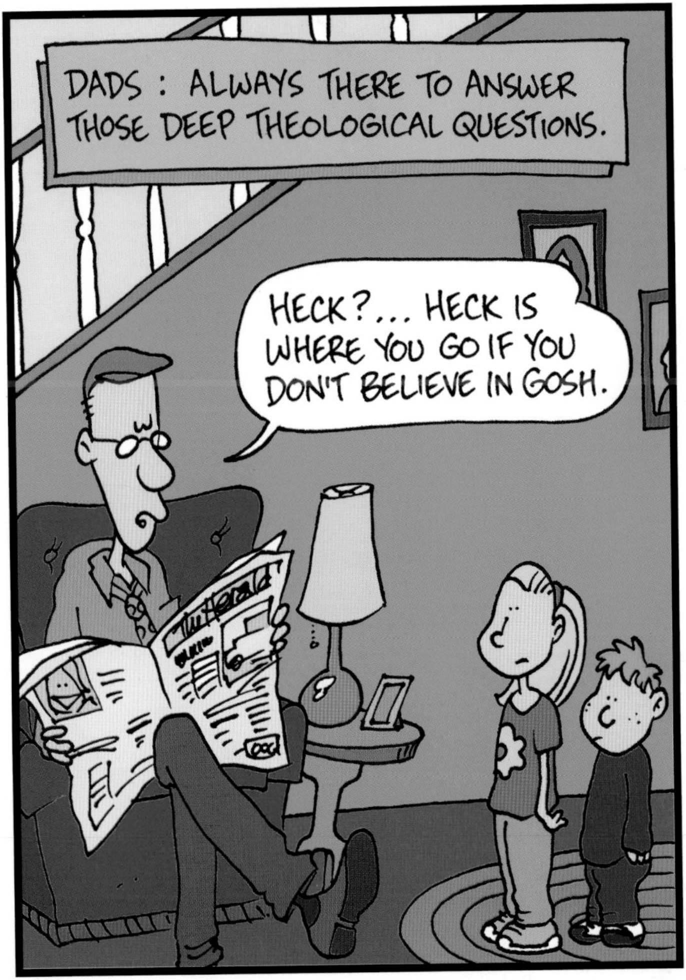
DADS : ALWAYS THERE TO ANSWER THOSE DEEP THEOLOGICAL QUESTIONS.
HECK?... HECK IS WHERE YOU GO IF YOU DON'T BELIEVE IN GOSH.
The Herald

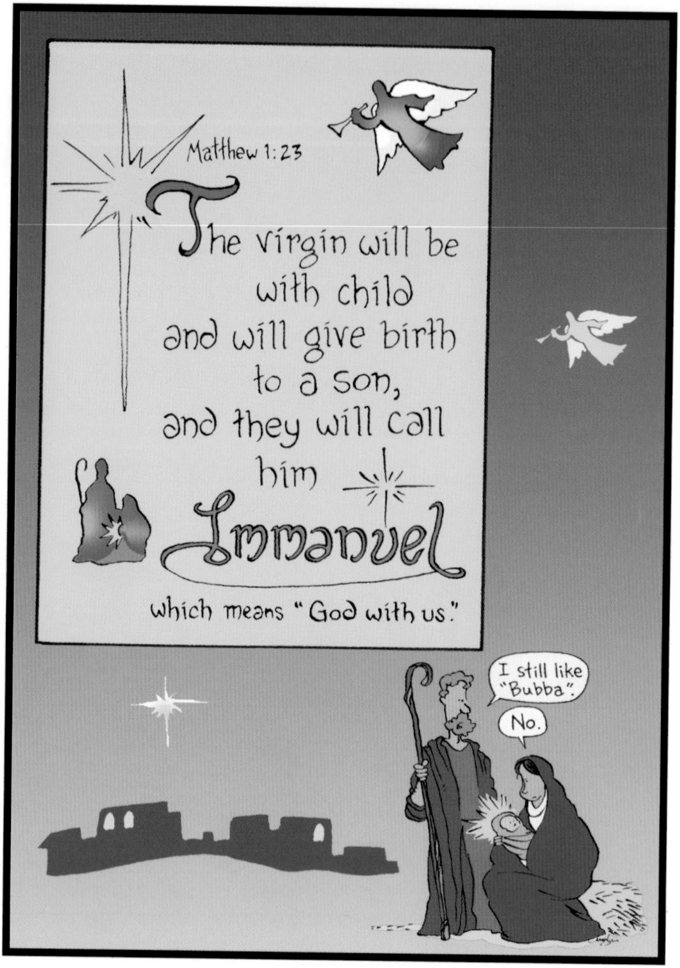
Matthew 1:23
"The virgin will be
with child
and will give birth
to a son,
and they will call
him
Immanuel
which means "God with us."
I still like "Bubba".
No.

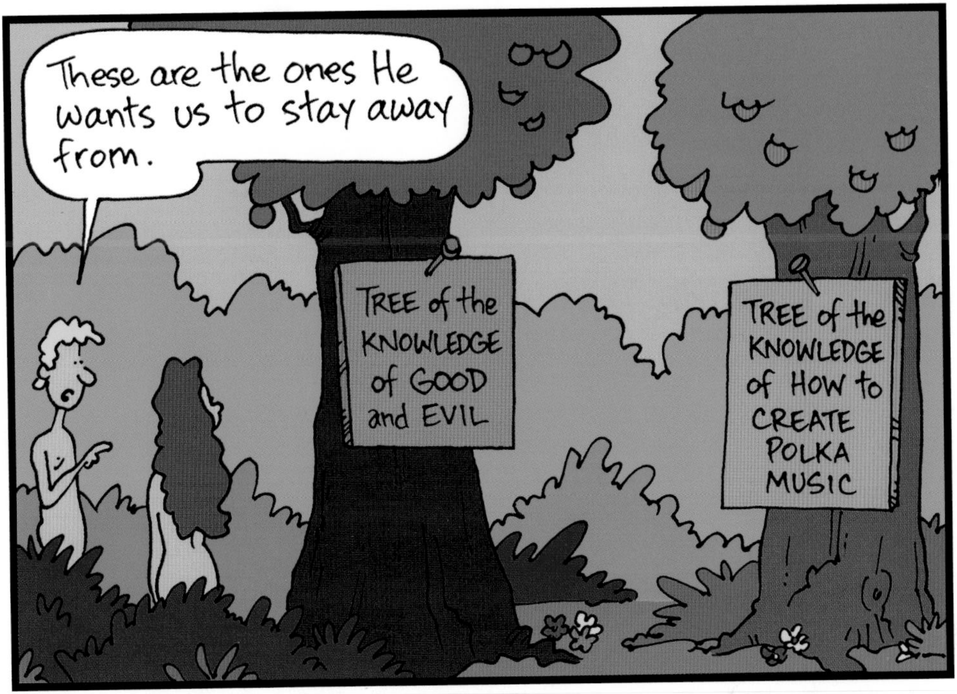
These are the ones He wants us to stay away from.
TREE of the KNOWLEDGE of GOOD and EVIL
TREE of the KNOWLEDGE of HOW to CREATE POLKA MUSIC

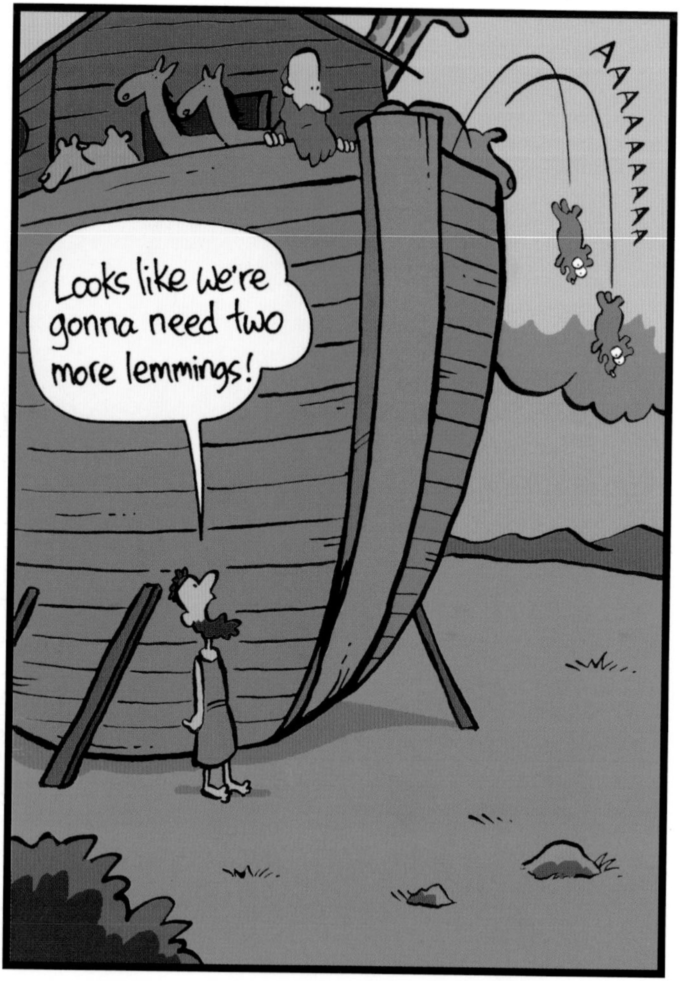
AAAAAAAAA
Looks like we're gonna need two more lemmings!

REV. BARNES HEADS OFF ON ANOTHER PASTORAL CALL.

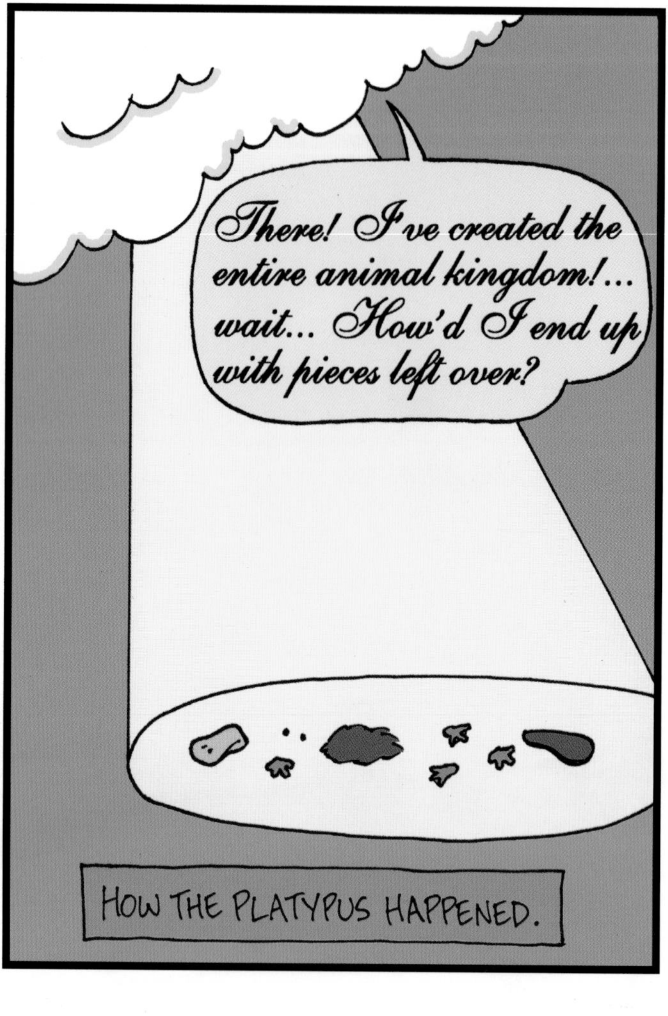
There! I've created the entire animal kingdom!... wait... How'd I end up with pieces left over?
HOW THE PLATYPUS HAPPENED.

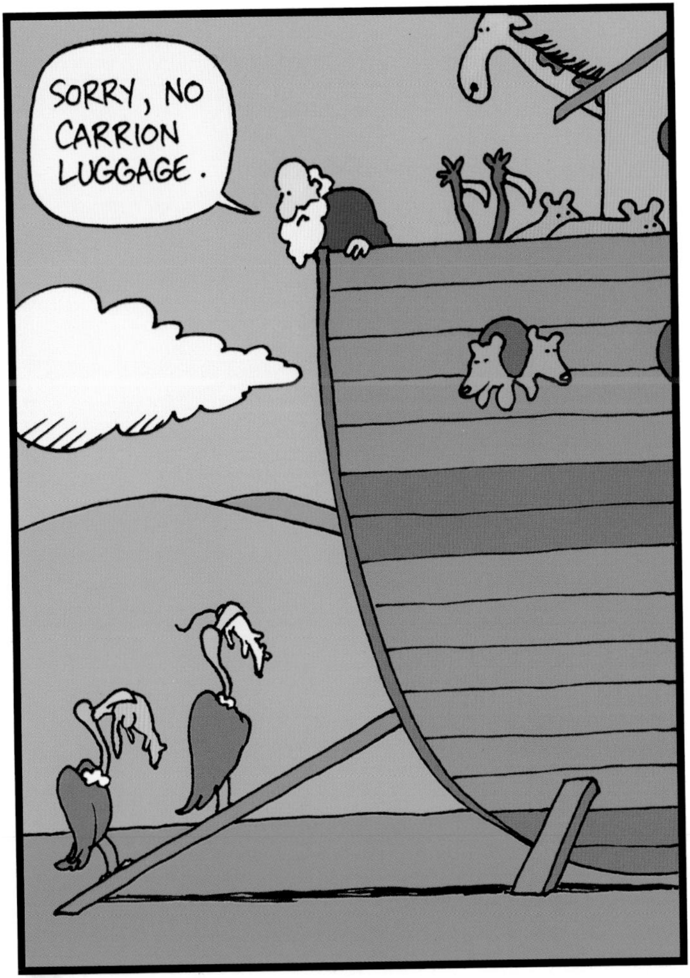
SORRY, NO CARRION LUGGAGE.

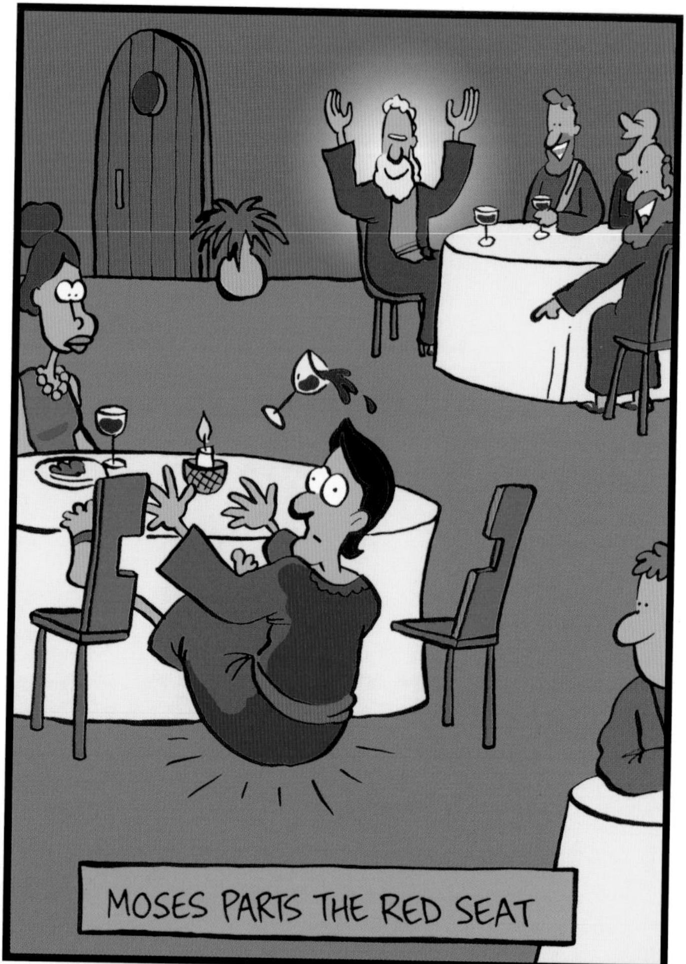
MOSES PARTS THE RED SEAT

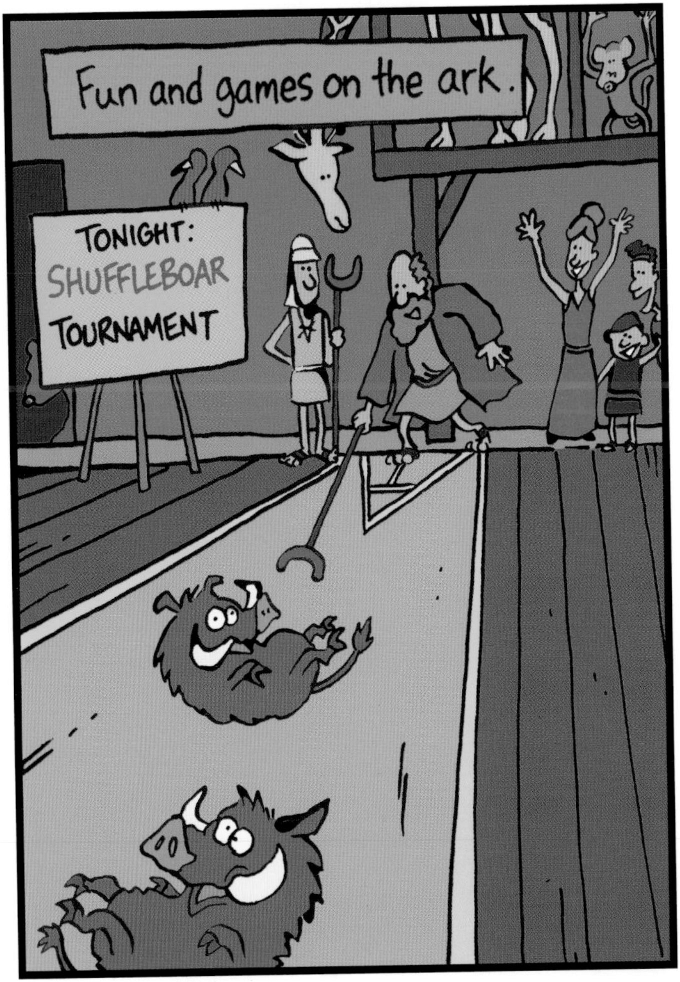
Fun and games on the ark.
TONIGHT:
SHUFFLEBOAR
TOURNAMENT

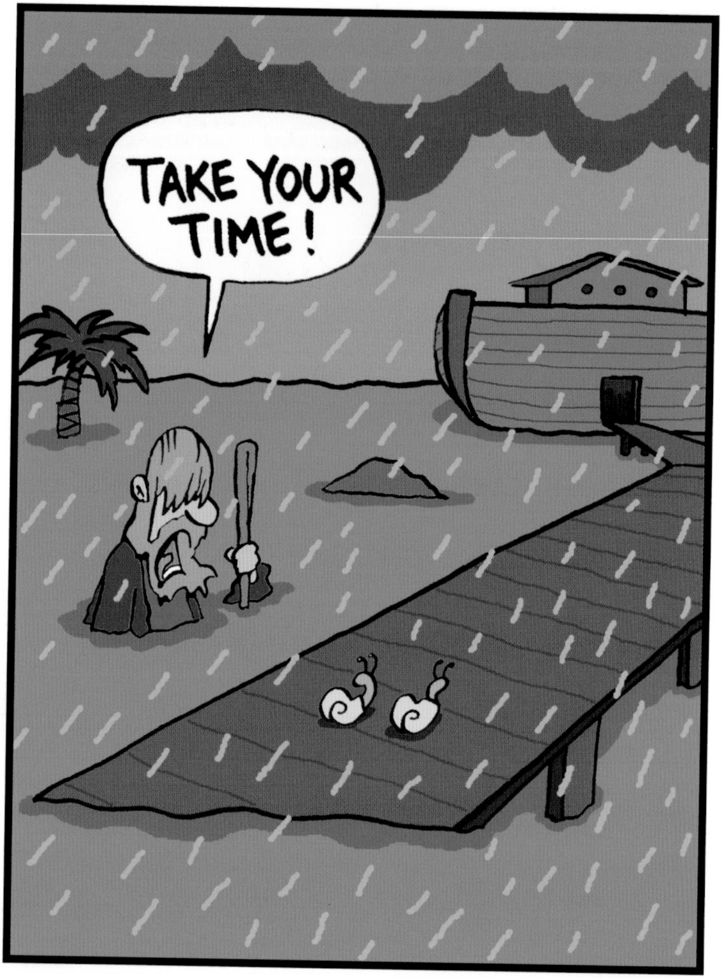
TAKE YOUR TIME!

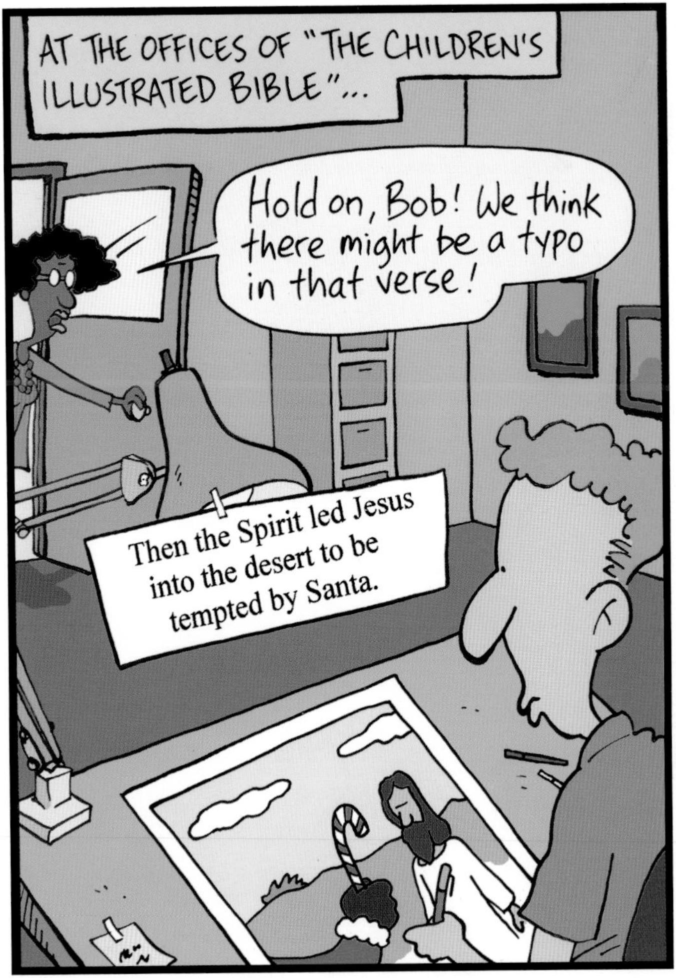
AT THE OFFICES OF "THE CHILDREN'S ILLUSTRATED BIBLE"...
Hold on, Bob! We think there might be a typo in that verse!
Then the Spirit led Jesus into the desert to be tempted by Santa.

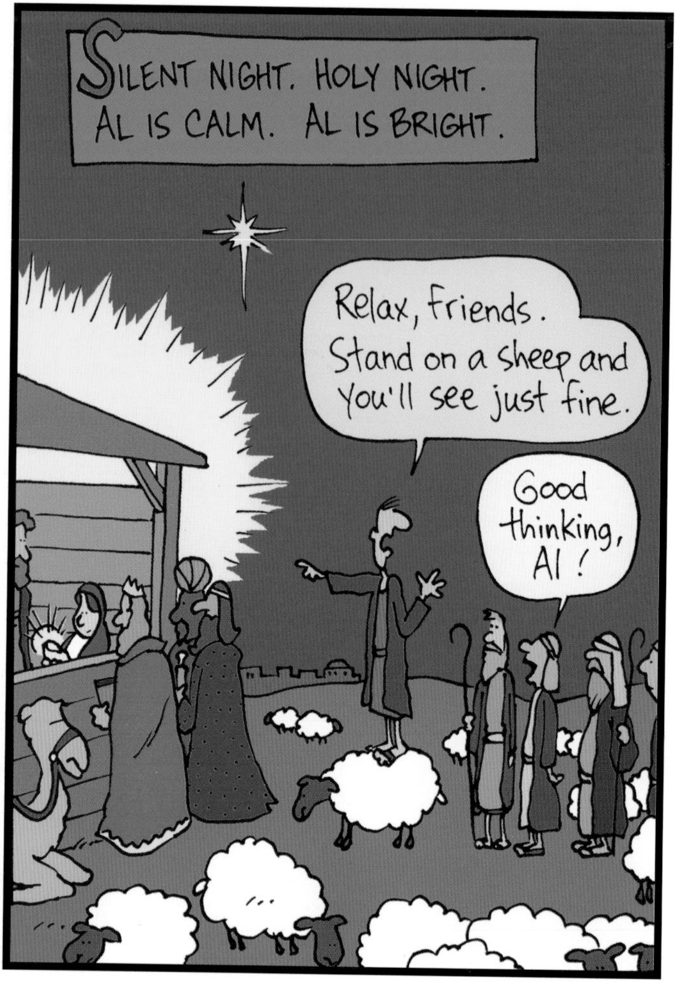
SILENT NIGHT. HOLY NIGHT.
AL IS CALM. AL IS BRIGHT.
Relax, friends. Stand on a sheep and you'll see just fine.
Good thinking, Al!

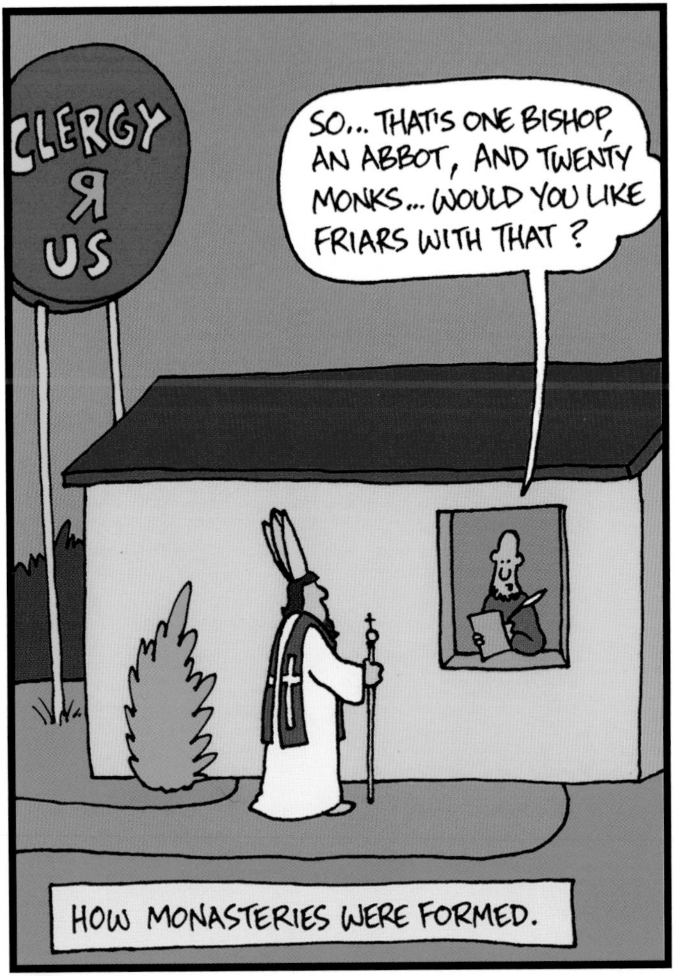
CLERGY Я US
SO... THAT'S ONE BISHOP, AN ABBOT, AND TWENTY MONKS... WOULD YOU LIKE FRIARS WITH THAT?
HOW MONASTERIES WERE FORMED.

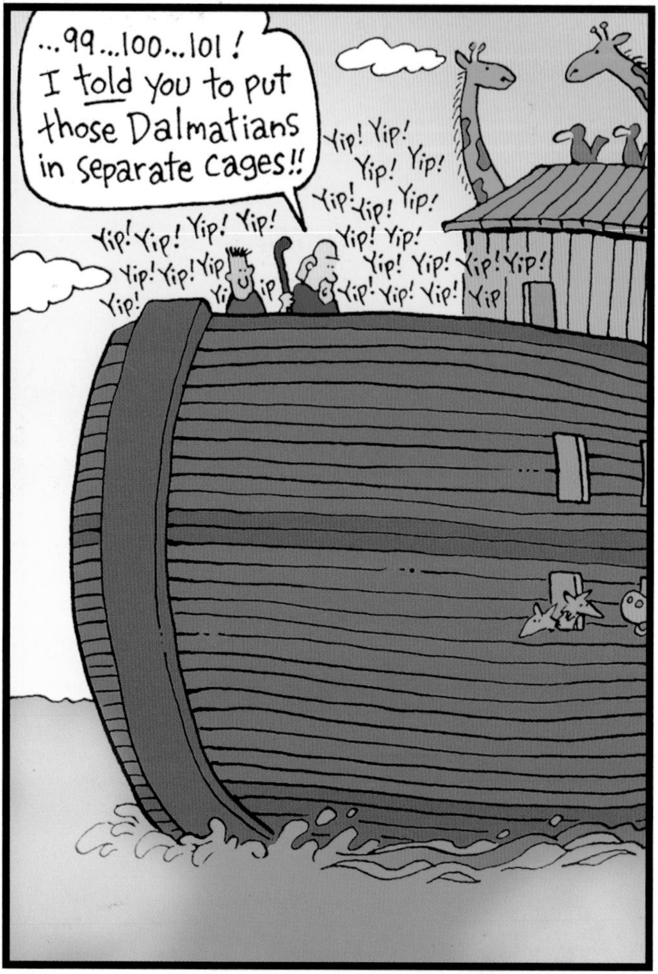
...99...100...101!
I told you to put those Dalmatians in separate cages!!
Yip! Yip! Yip! Yip! Yip! Yip! Yip! Yip! Yip! Yip! Yip! Yip! Yip! Yip! Yip! Yip! Yip! Yip! Yip! Yip! Yip! Yip! Yip! Yip!

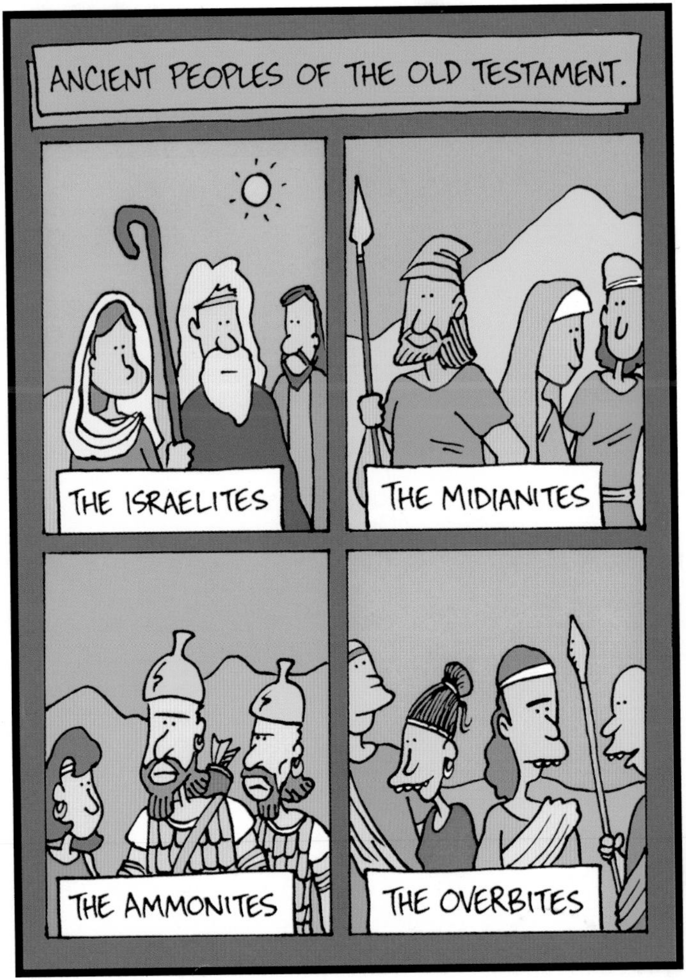
ANCIENT PEOPLES OF THE OLD TESTAMENT.
THE ISRAELITES
THE MIDIANITES
THE AMMONITES
THE OVERBITES

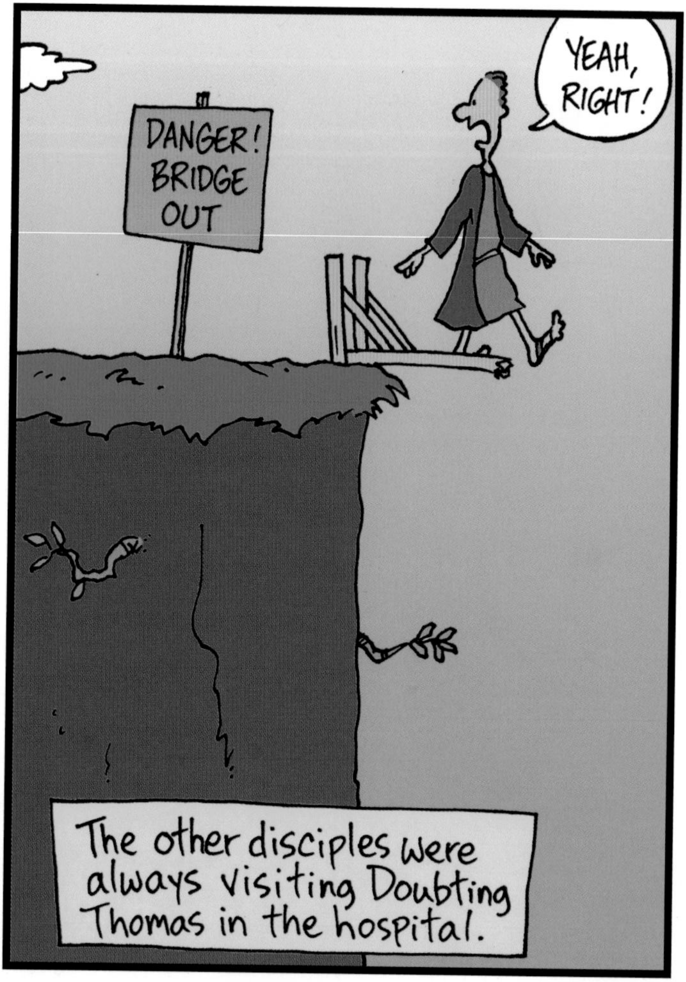
DANGER! BRIDGE OUT
YEAH, RIGHT!
The other disciples were always visiting Doubting Thomas in the hospital.

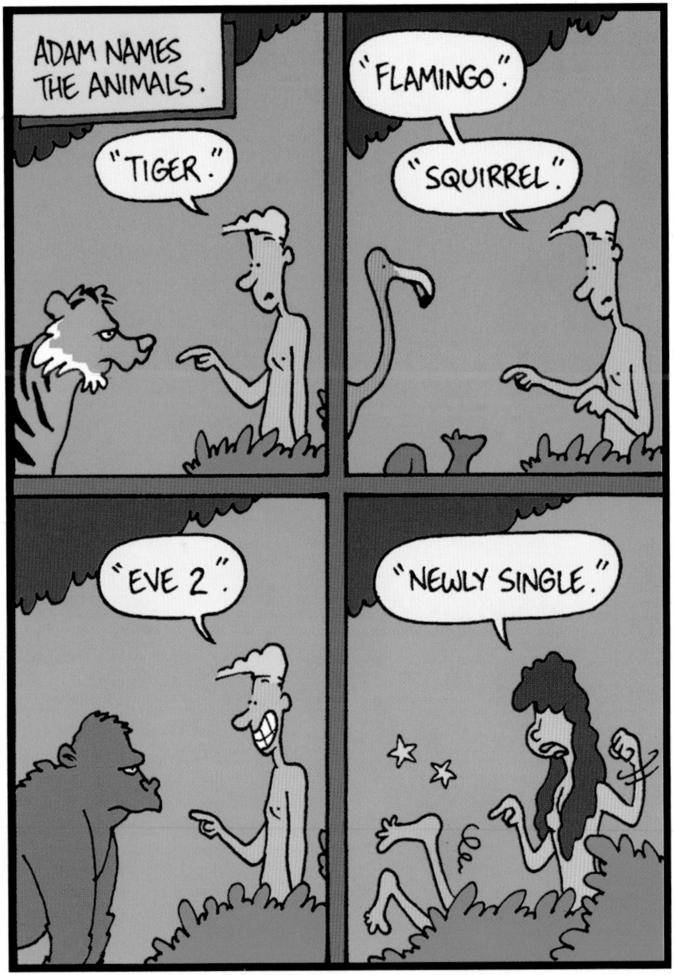
ADAM NAMES THE ANIMALS.
"TIGER."
"FLAMINGO."
"SQUIRREL."
"EVE 2."
"NEWLY SINGLE."

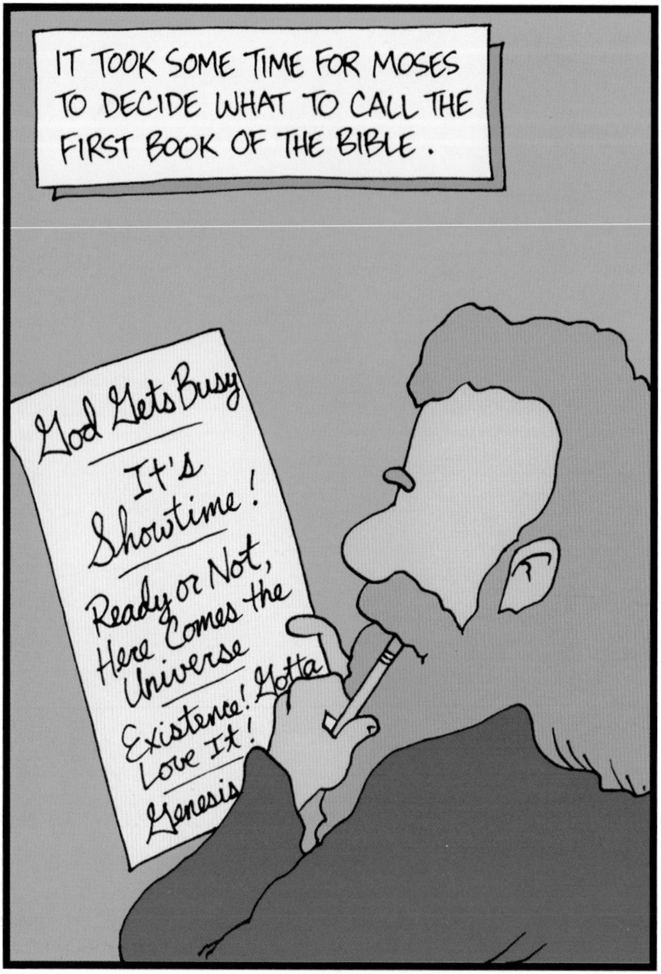
IT TOOK SOME TIME FOR MOSES TO DECIDE WHAT TO CALL THE FIRST BOOK OF THE BIBLE.
God Gets Busy
It's Showtime!
Ready or Not, Here Comes the Universe
Existence! Gotta Love It!
Genesis

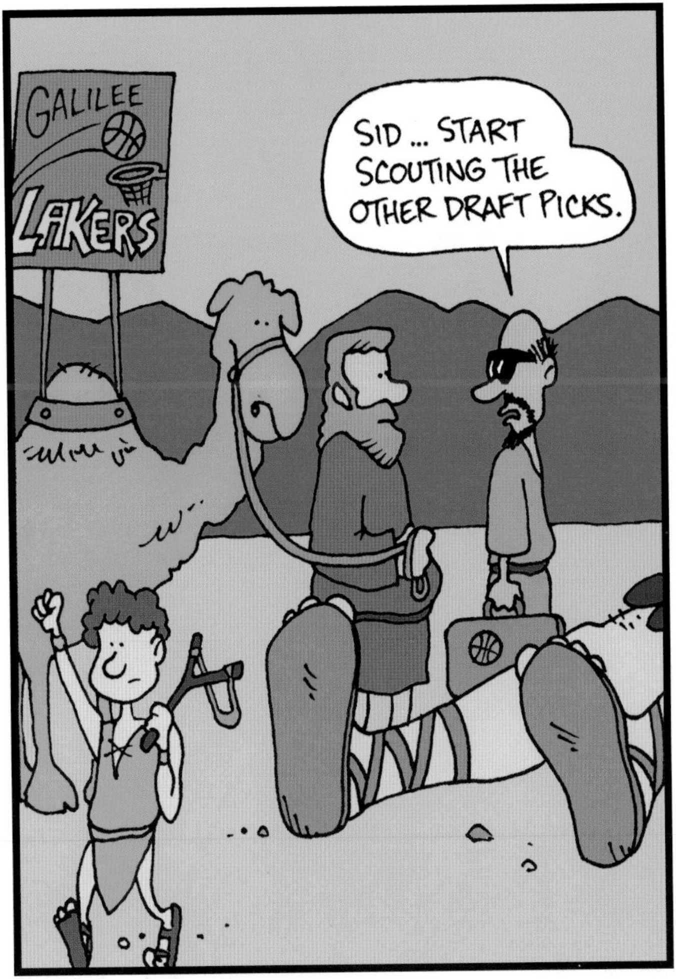
GALILEE
LAKERS
SID ... START SCOUTING THE OTHER DRAFT PICKS.

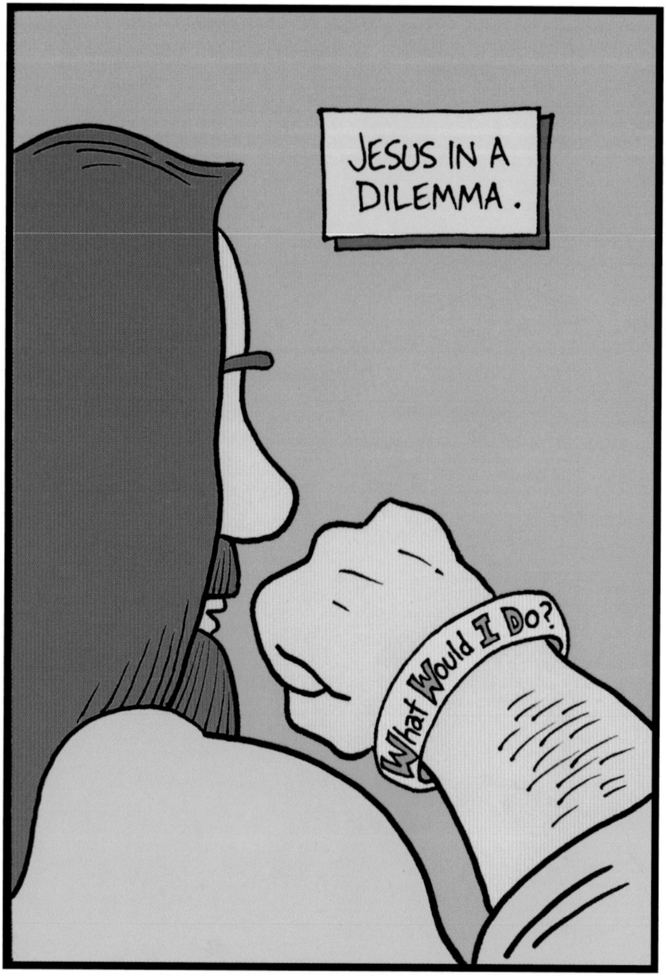
JESUS IN A DILEMMA.
What Would I Do?

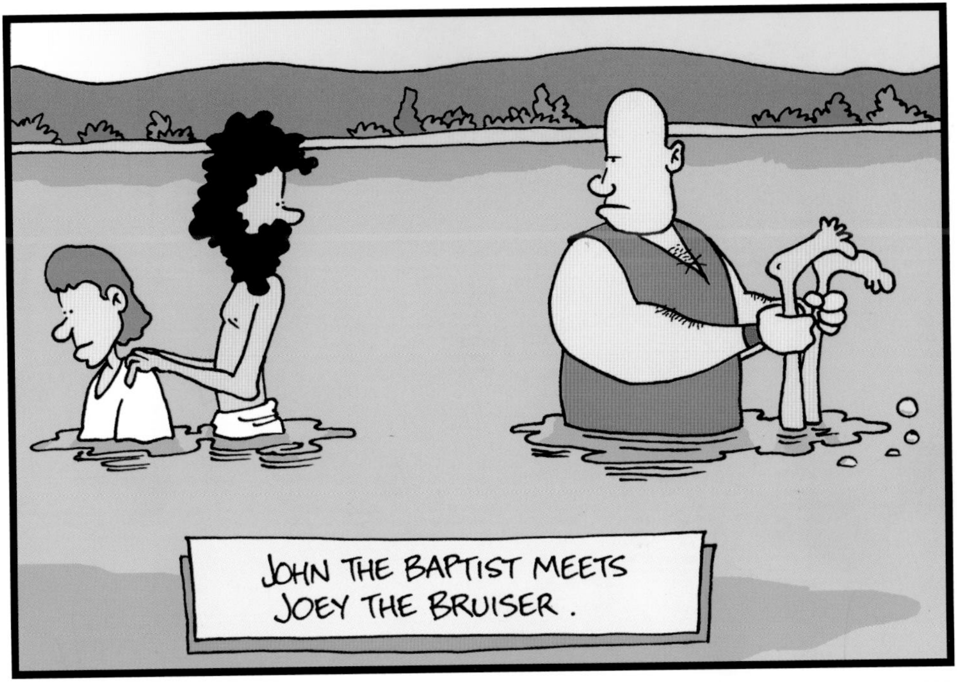
JOHN THE BAPTIST MEETS JOEY THE BRUISER.

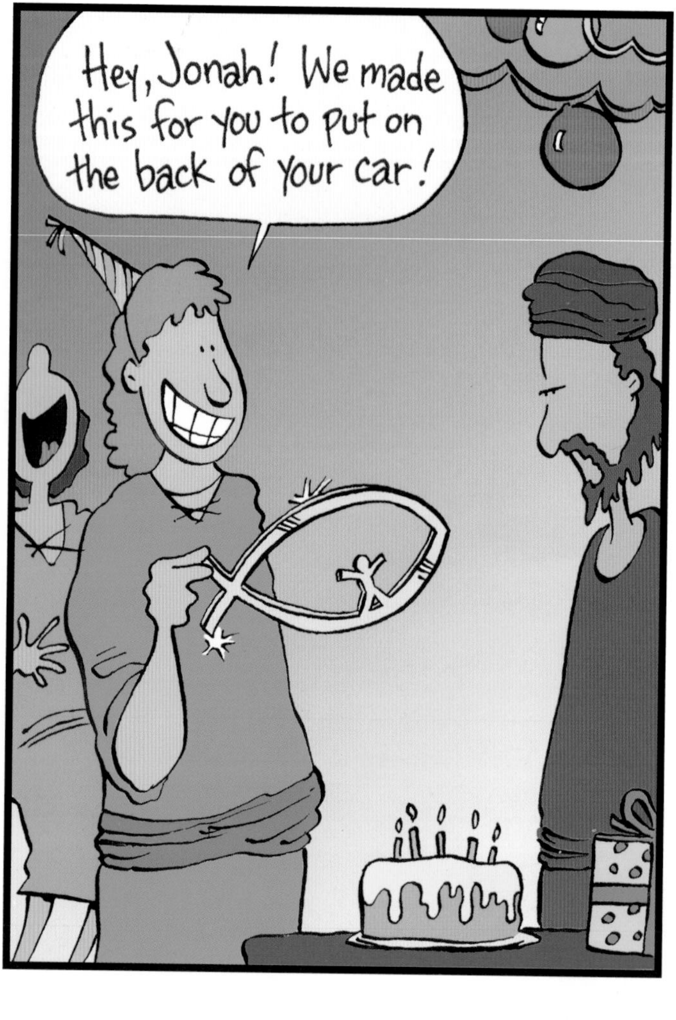
Hey, Jonah! We made this for you to put on the back of your car!

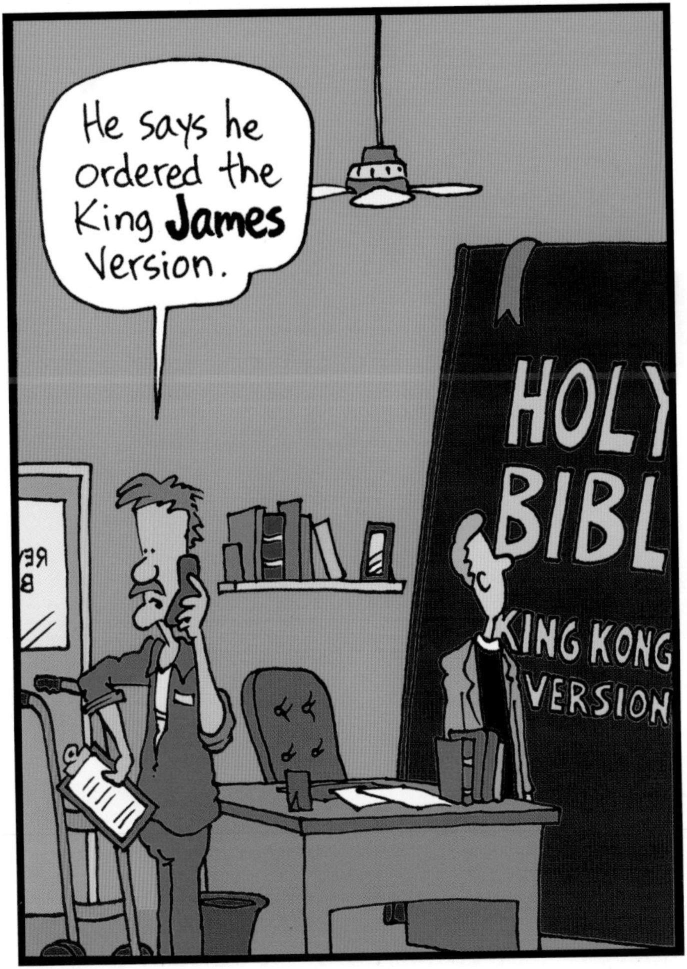
He says he ordered the King **James** Version.
HOLY
BIBL
KING KONG
VERSION

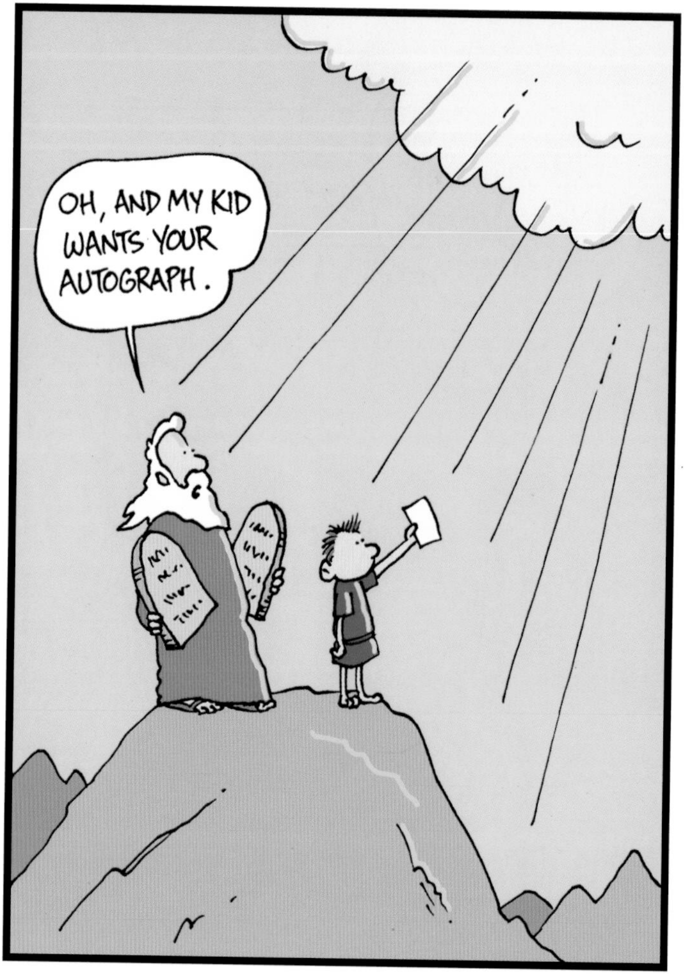
OH, AND MY KID WANTS YOUR AUTOGRAPH.

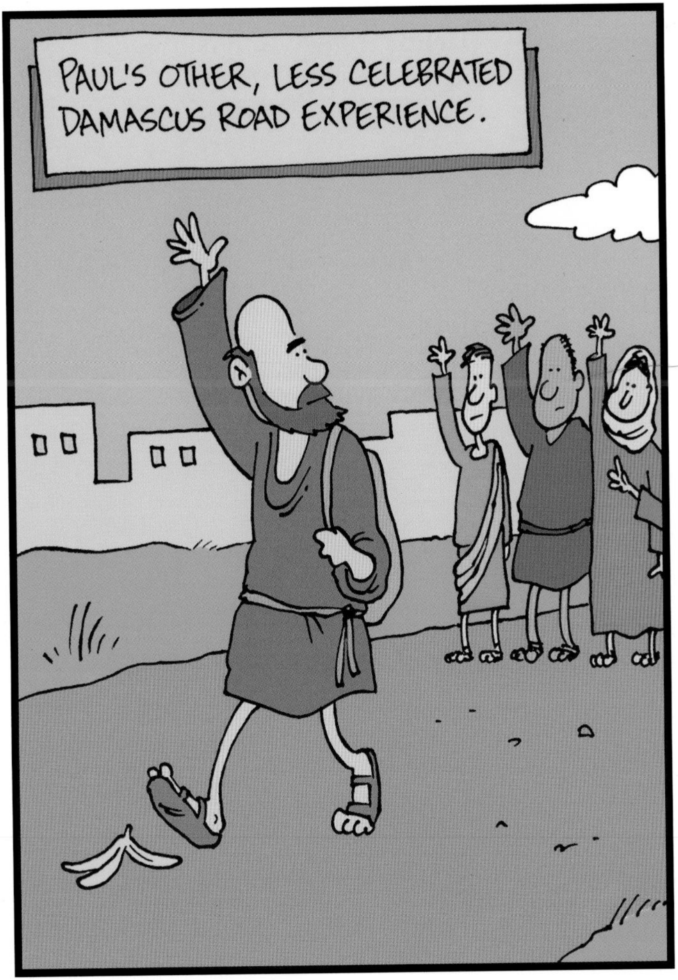
PAUL'S OTHER, LESS CELEBRATED
DAMASCUS ROAD EXPERIENCE.

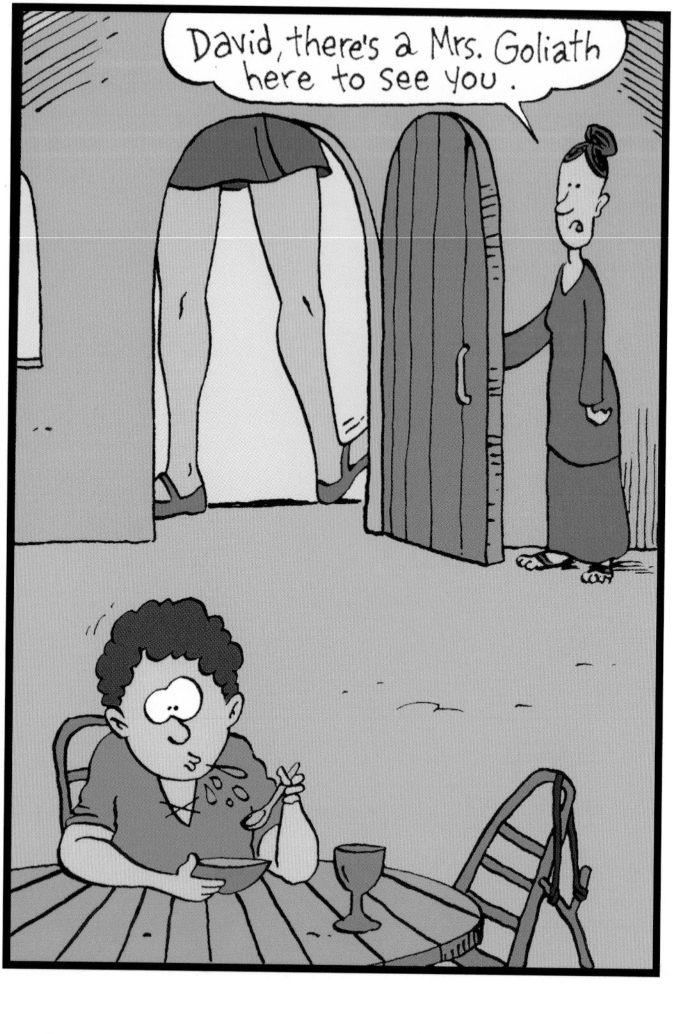
David, there's a Mrs. Goliath here to see you.

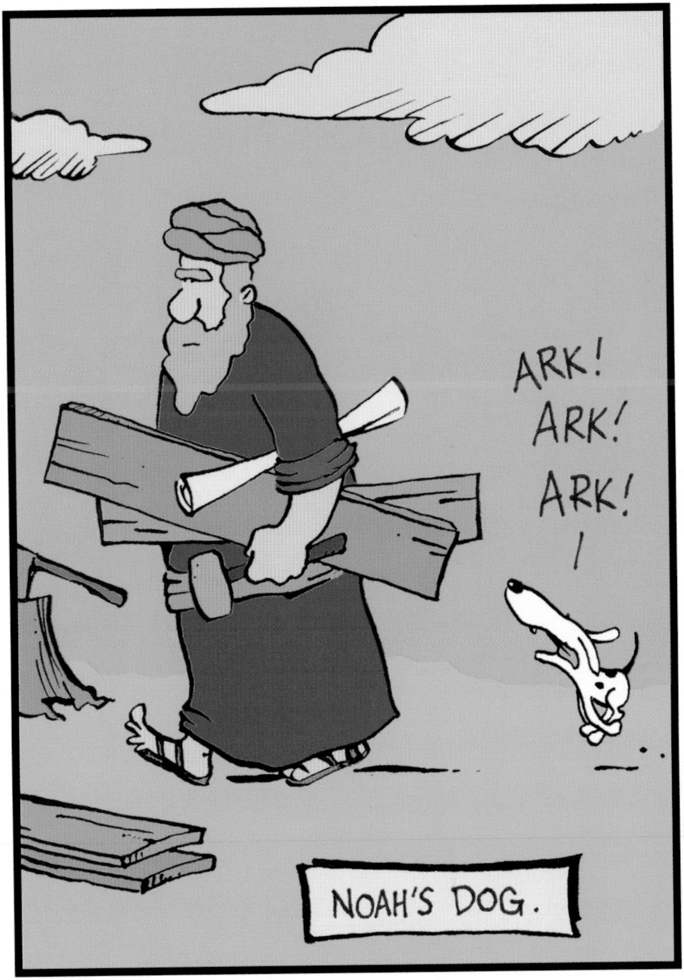
ARK! ARK! ARK!
NOAH'S DOG.

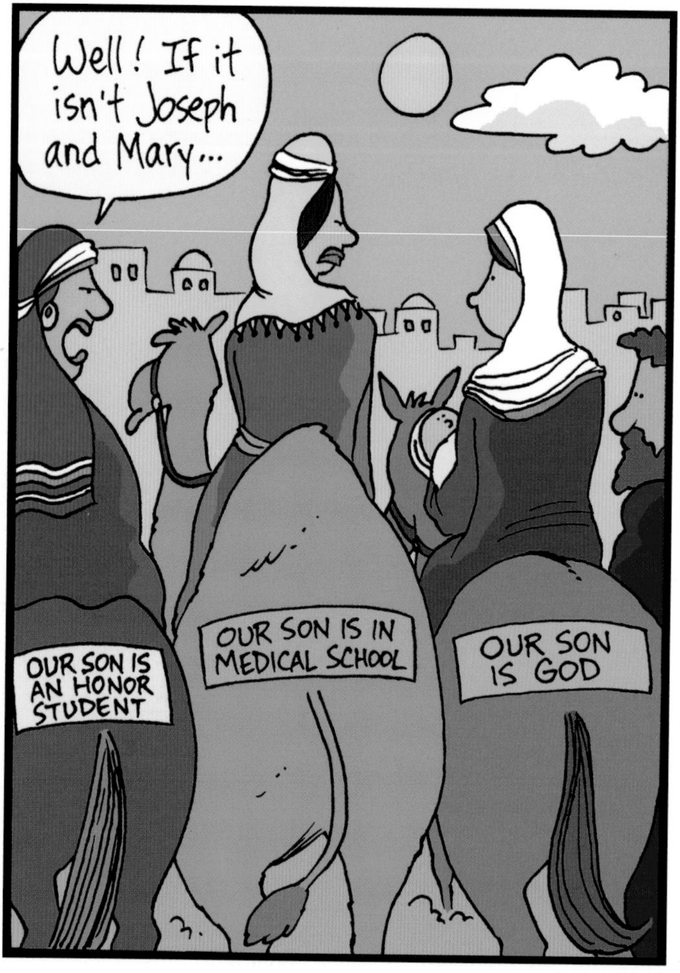
Well! If it isn't Joseph and Mary...
OUR SON IS AN HONOR STUDENT
OUR SON IS IN MEDICAL SCHOOL
OUR SON IS GOD

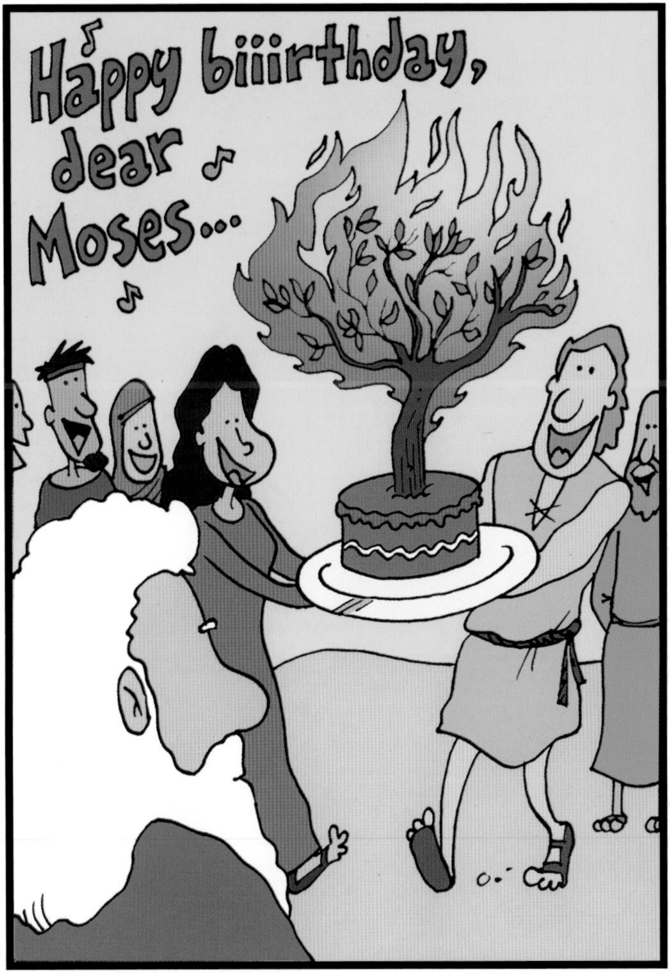
Happy biiirthday, dear Moses...

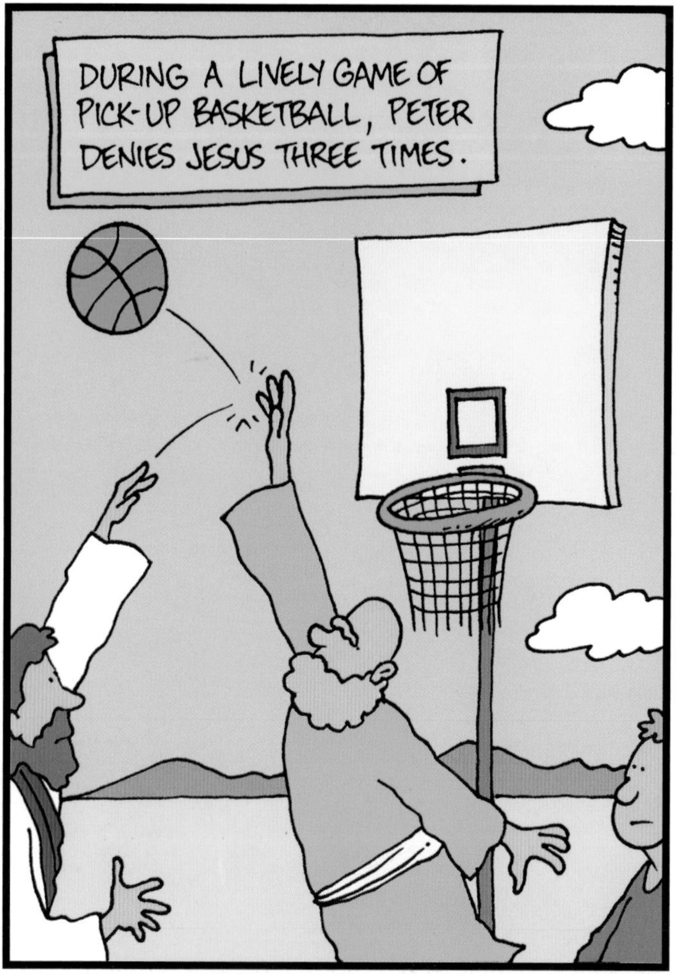
DURING A LIVELY GAME OF PICK-UP BASKETBALL, PETER DENIES JESUS THREE TIMES.

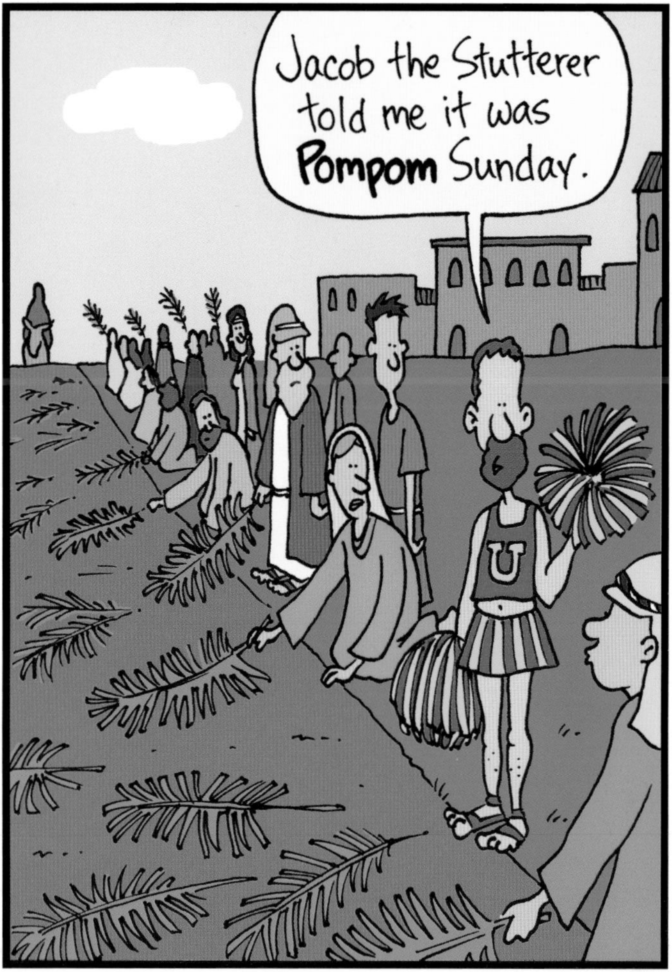
Jacob the Stutterer told me it was **Pompom** Sunday.

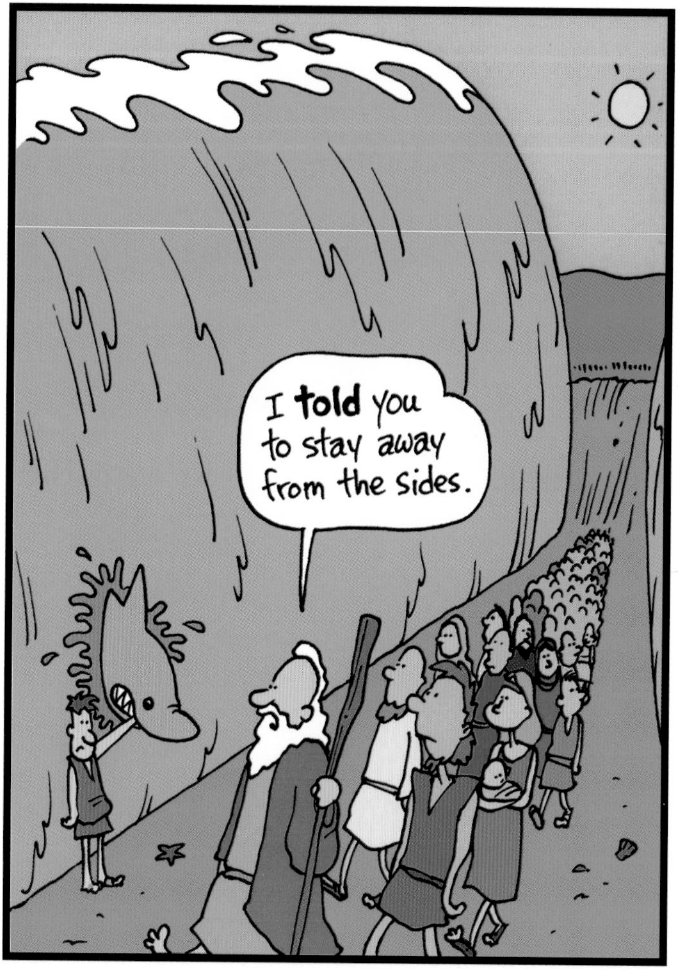
I **told** you to stay away from the sides.

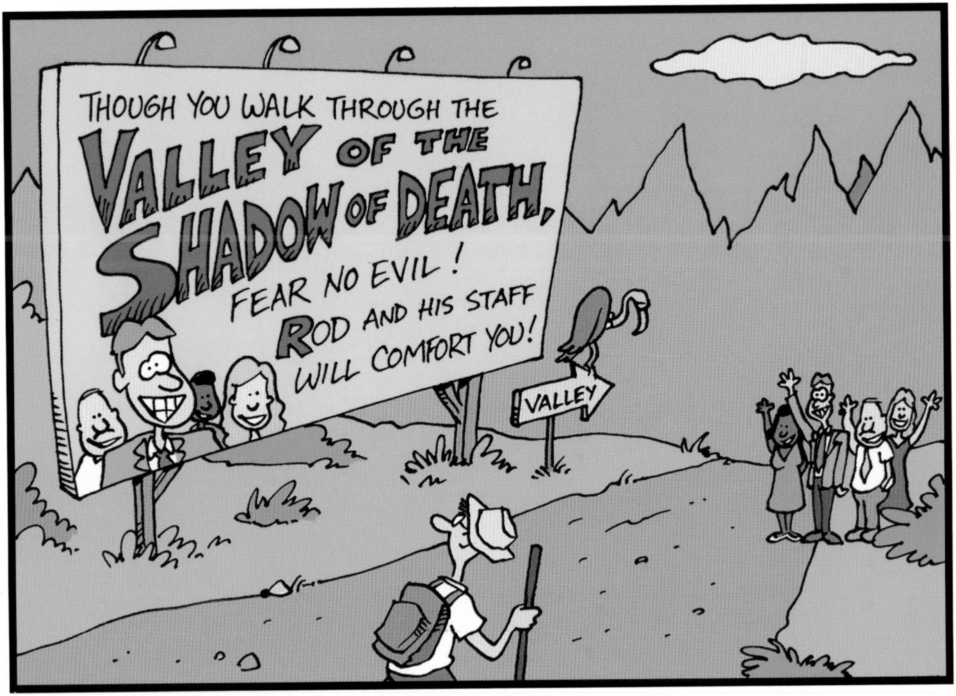

THOUGH YOU WALK THROUGH THE
VALLEY OF THE
SHADOW OF DEATH,
FEAR NO EVIL!
ROD AND HIS STAFF
WILL COMFORT YOU!
VALLEY

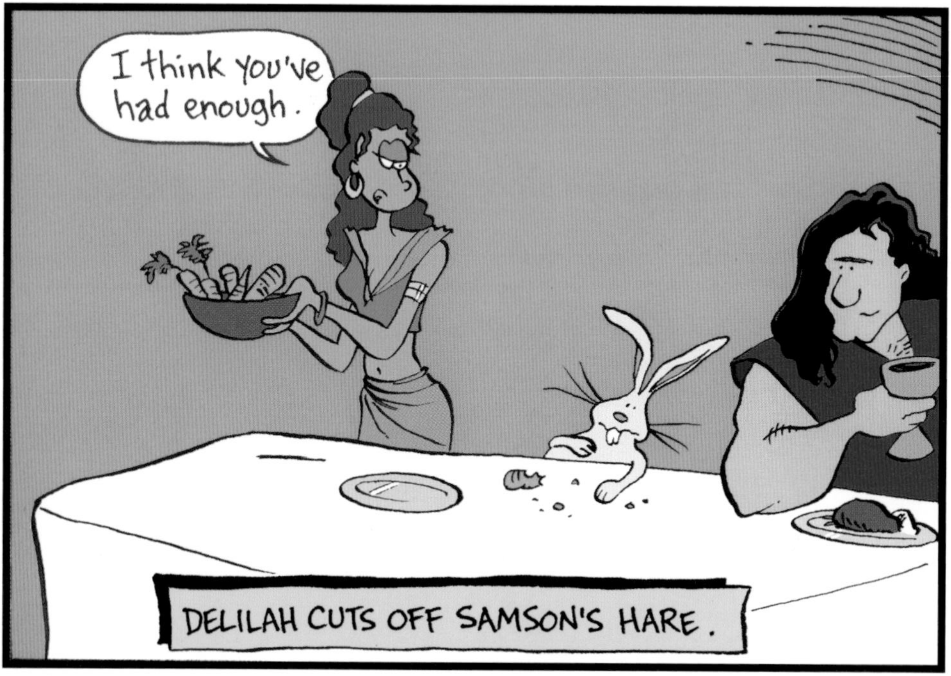
I think you've had enough.
DELILAH CUTS OFF SAMSON'S HARE.

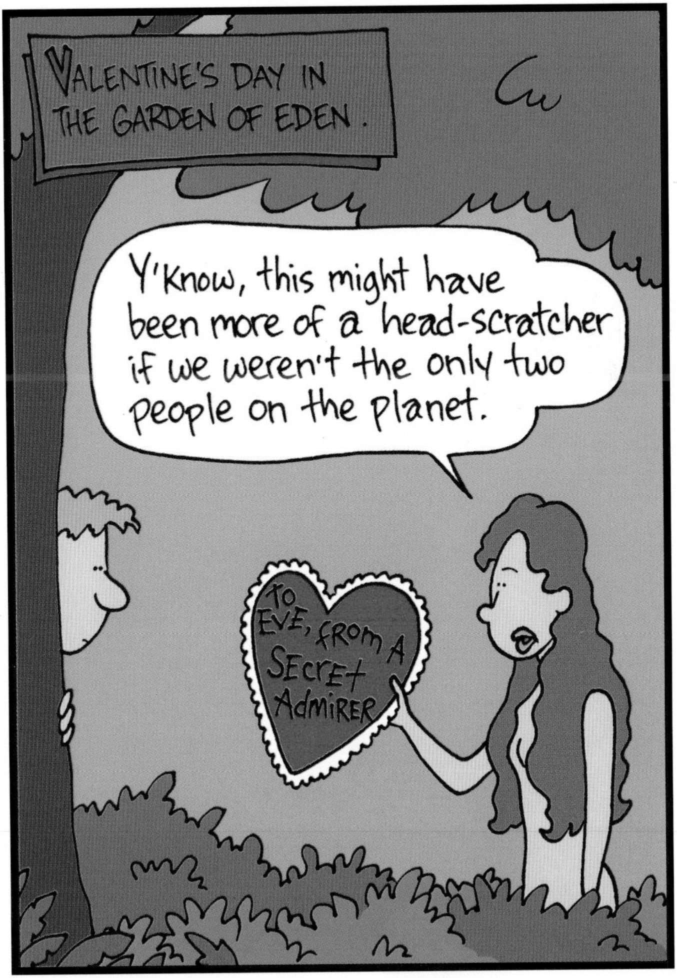
VALENTINE'S DAY IN THE GARDEN OF EDEN.
Y'Know, this might have been more of a head-scratcher if we weren't the only two people on the planet.
TO EVE, FROM A SECRET ADMIRER

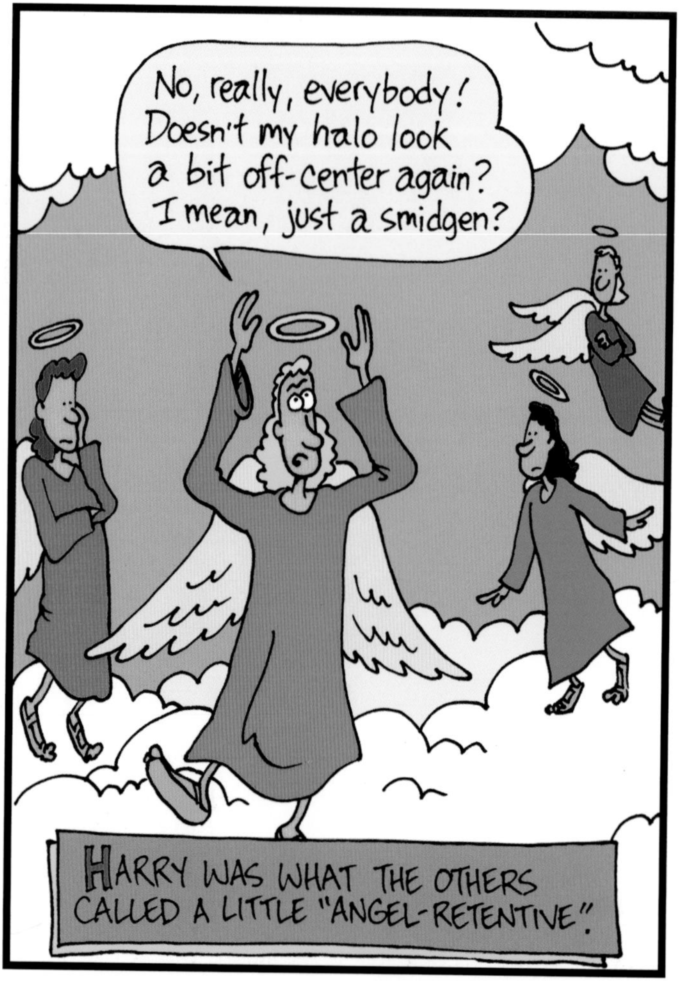
No, really, everybody! Doesn't my halo look a bit off-center again? I mean, just a smidgen?
HARRY WAS WHAT THE OTHERS CALLED A LITTLE "ANGEL-RETENTIVE".

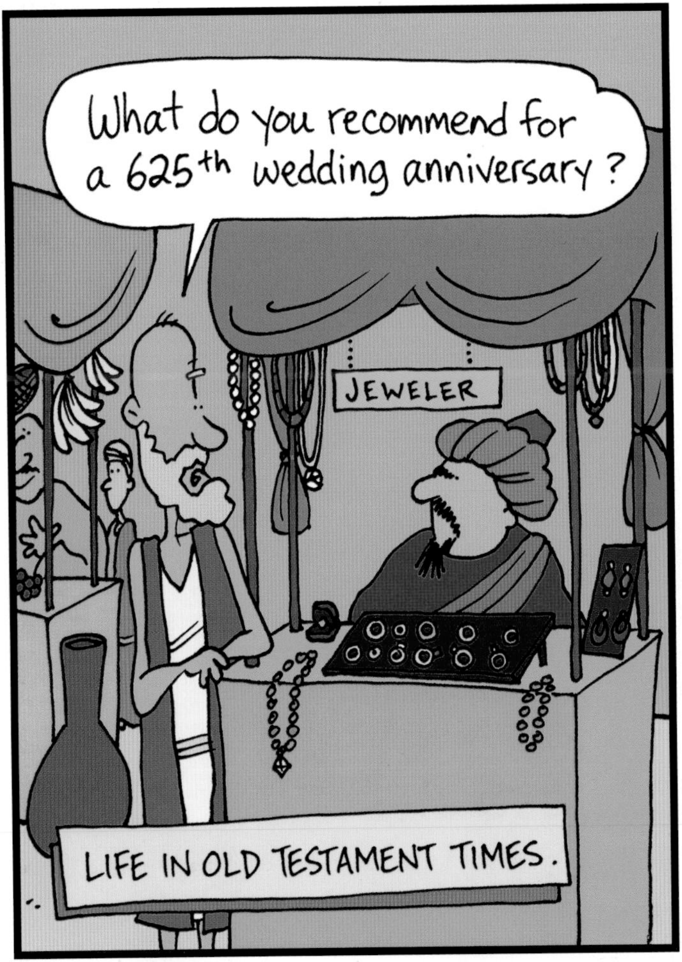
What do you recommend for a 625th wedding anniversary?
JEWELER
LIFE IN OLD TESTAMENT TIMES.

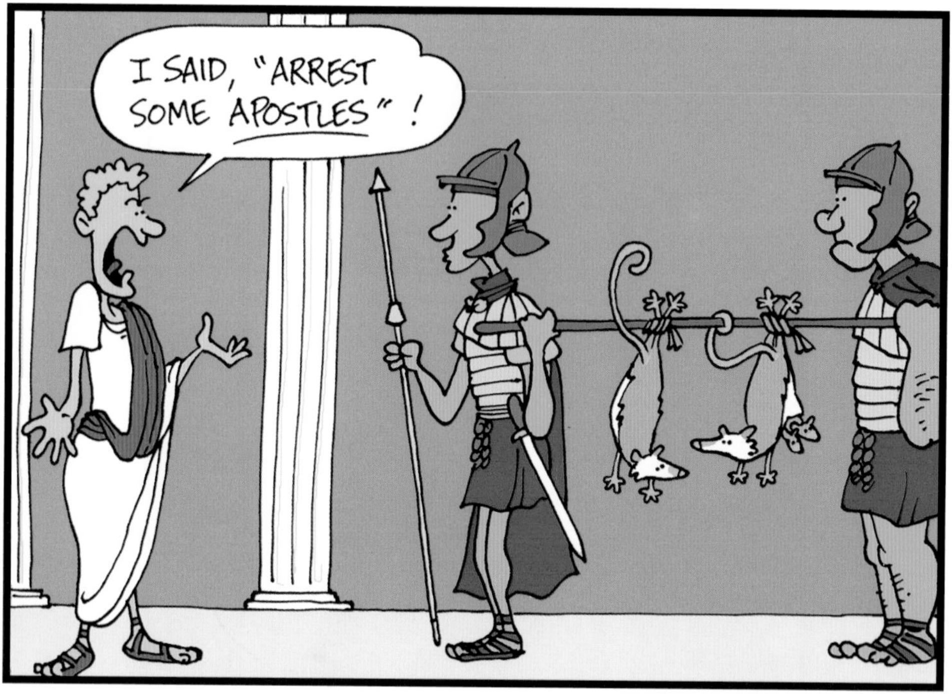
I SAID, "ARREST SOME APOSTLES"!

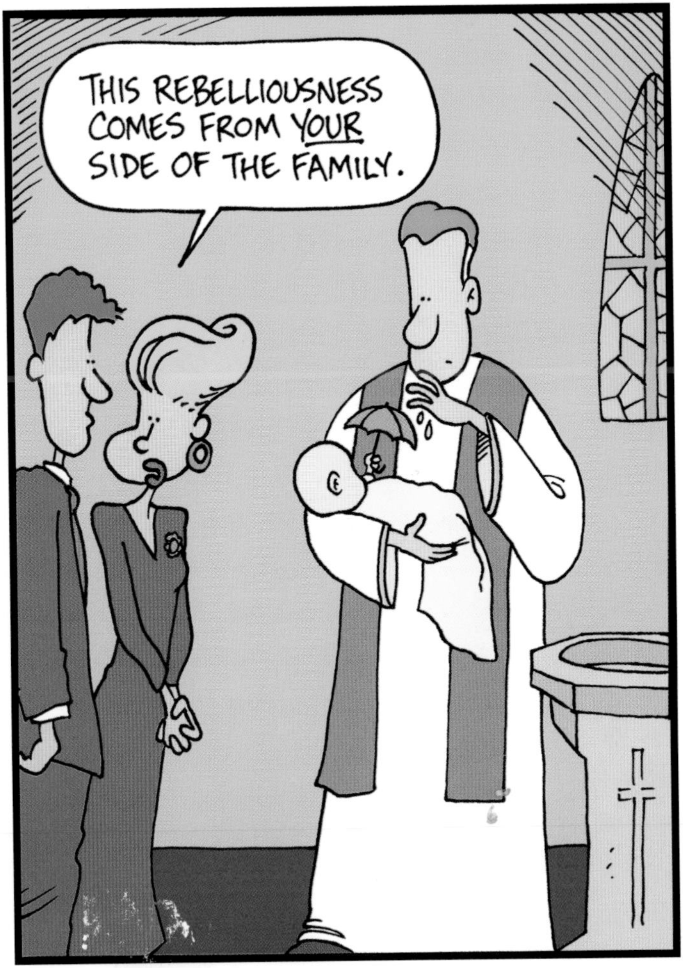
THIS REBELLIOUSNESS COMES FROM YOUR SIDE OF THE FAMILY.

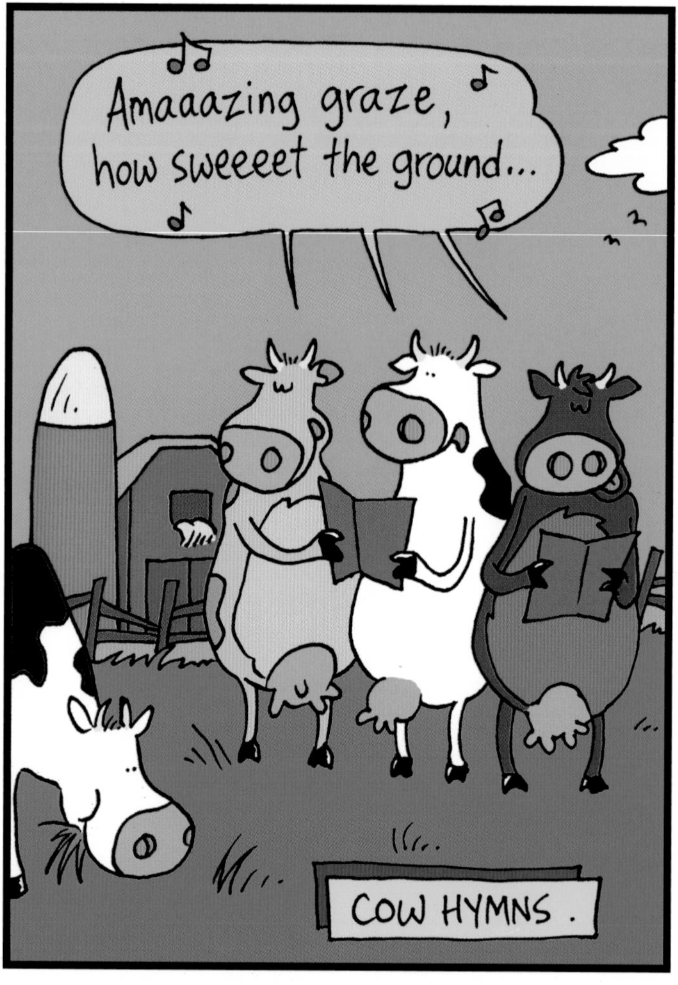
Amaaazing graze, how sweeeet the ground...
COW HYMNS.

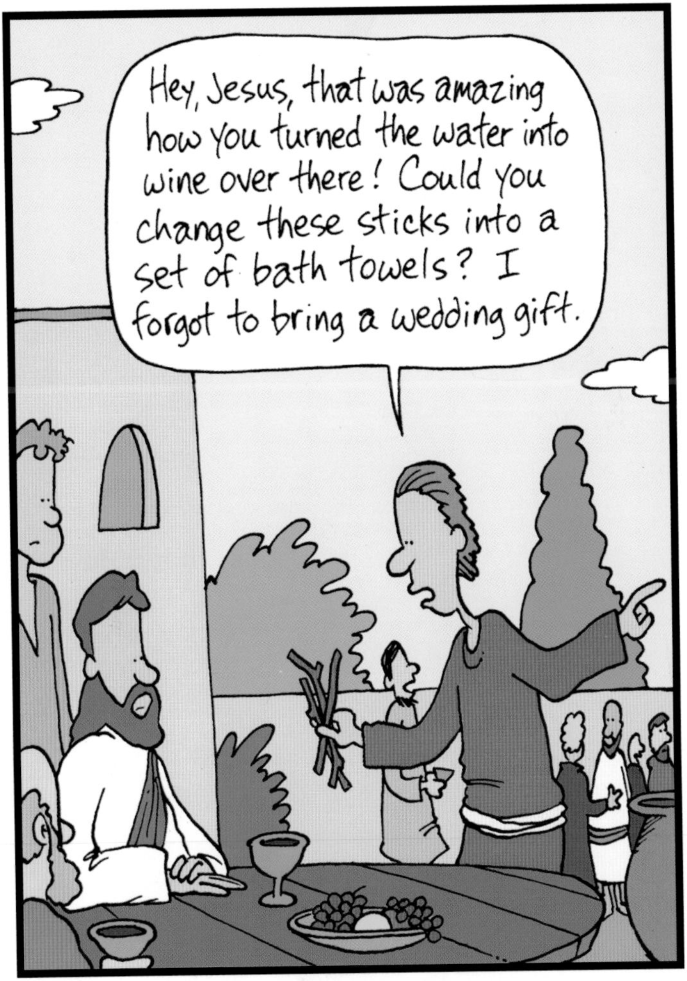
Hey, Jesus, that was amazing how you turned the water into wine over there! Could you change these sticks into a set of bath towels? I forgot to bring a wedding gift.

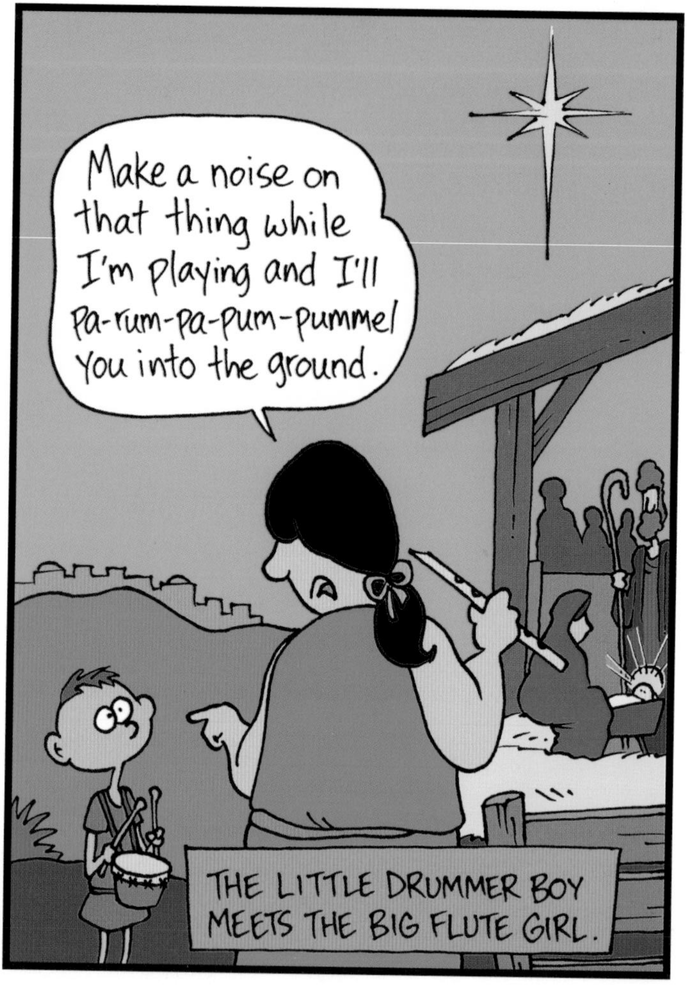
Make a noise on that thing while I'm playing and I'll pa-rum-pa-pum-pummel you into the ground.
THE LITTLE DRUMMER BOY MEETS THE BIG FLUTE GIRL.

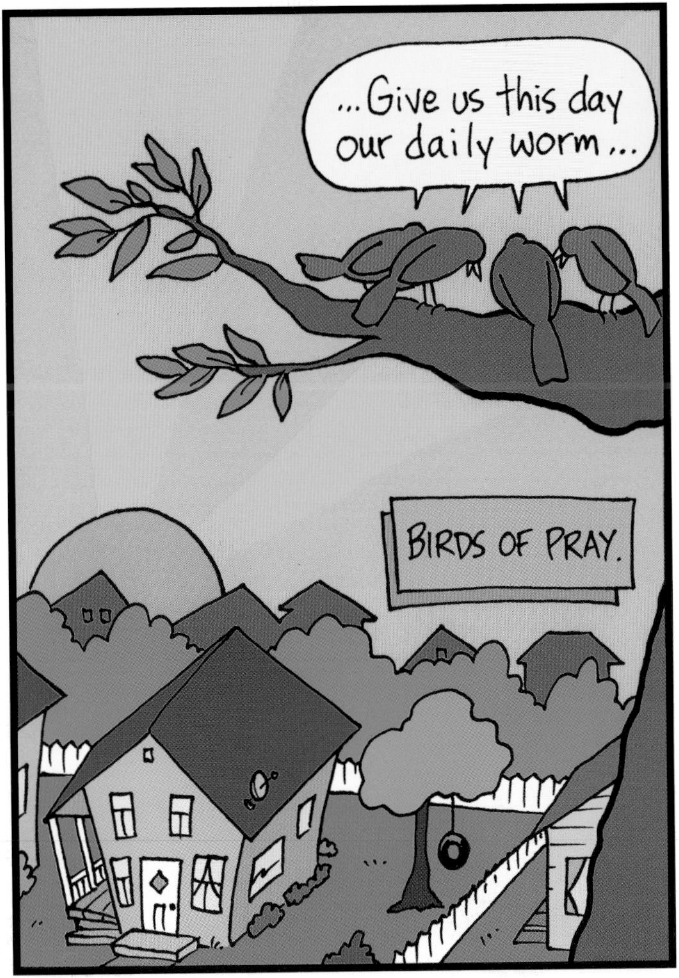
...Give us this day our daily worm...
BIRDS OF PRAY.

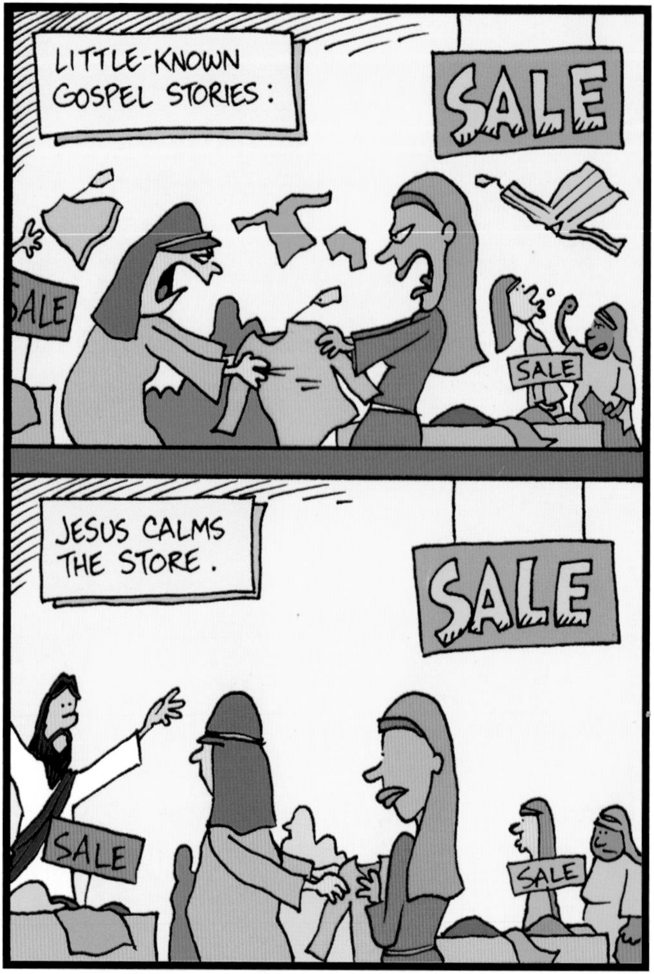
LITTLE-KNOWN GOSPEL STORIES:
SALE
SALE
SALE
JESUS CALMS THE STORE.
SALE
SALE
SALE

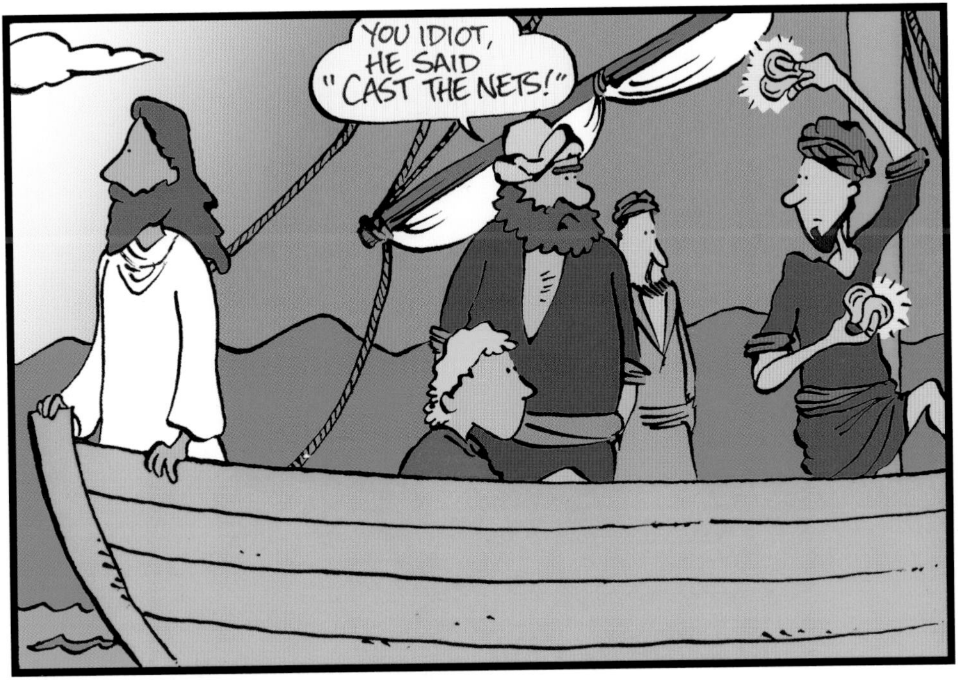
YOU IDIOT, HE SAID "CAST THE NETS!"

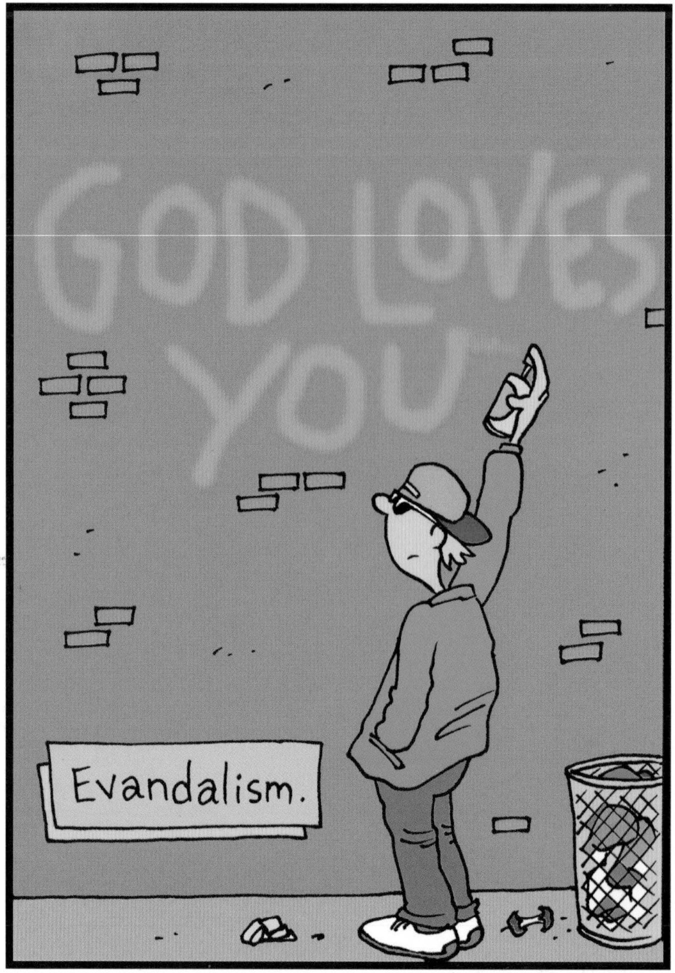
GOD LOVES YOU
Evandalism.

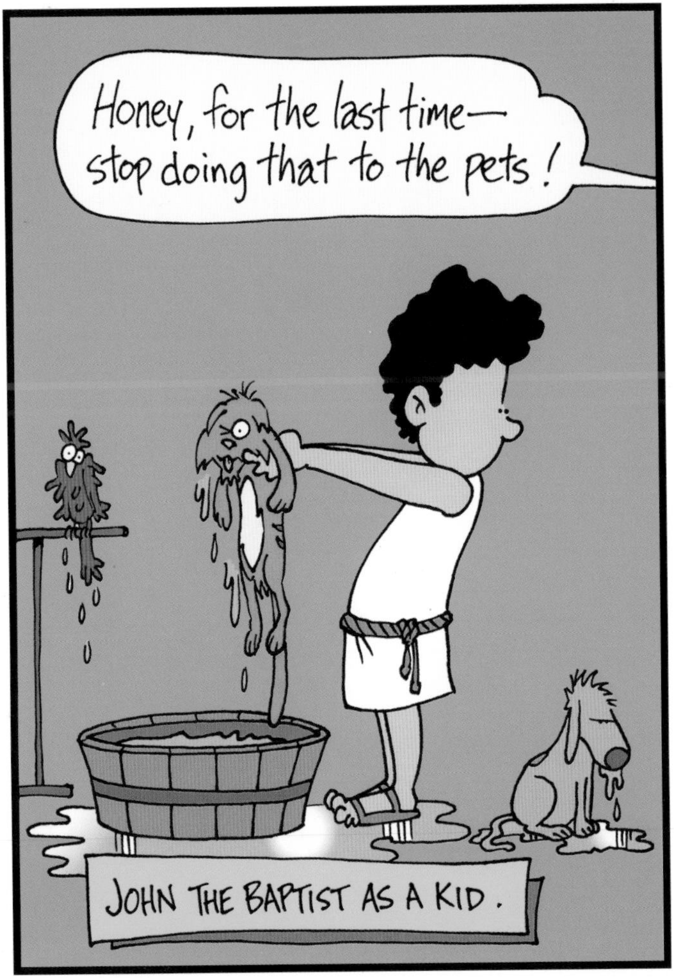
Honey, for the last time— stop doing that to the pets!
JOHN THE BAPTIST AS A KID.

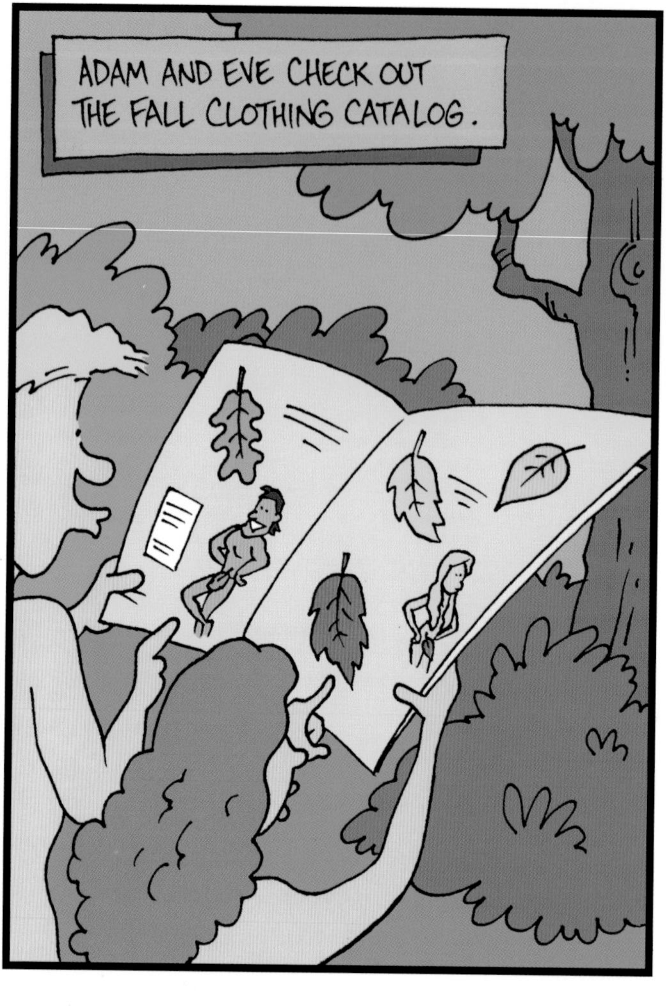
ADAM AND EVE CHECK OUT THE FALL CLOTHING CATALOG.

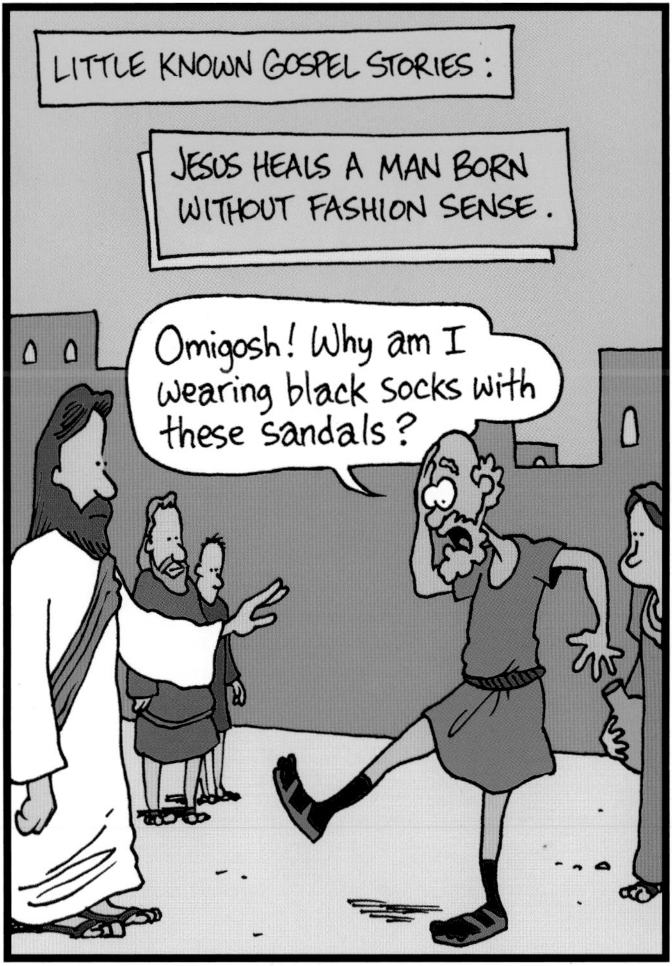
LITTLE KNOWN GOSPEL STORIES:
JESUS HEALS A MAN BORN WITHOUT FASHION SENSE.
Omigosh! Why am I wearing black socks with these sandals?

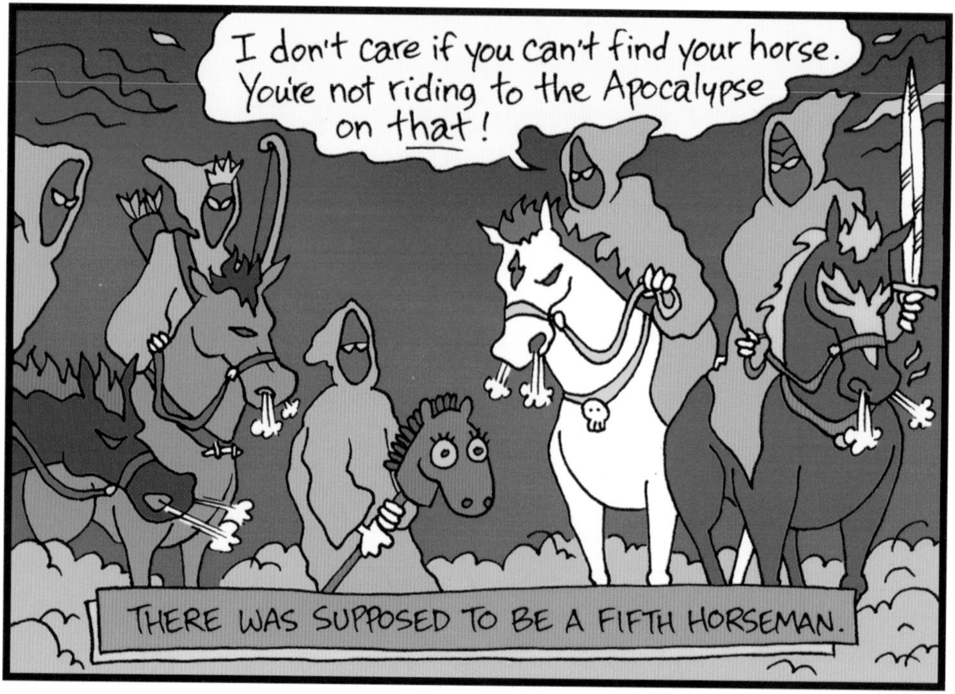
I don't care if you can't find your horse. You're not riding to the Apocalypse on that!
THERE WAS SUPPOSED TO BE A FIFTH HORSEMAN.

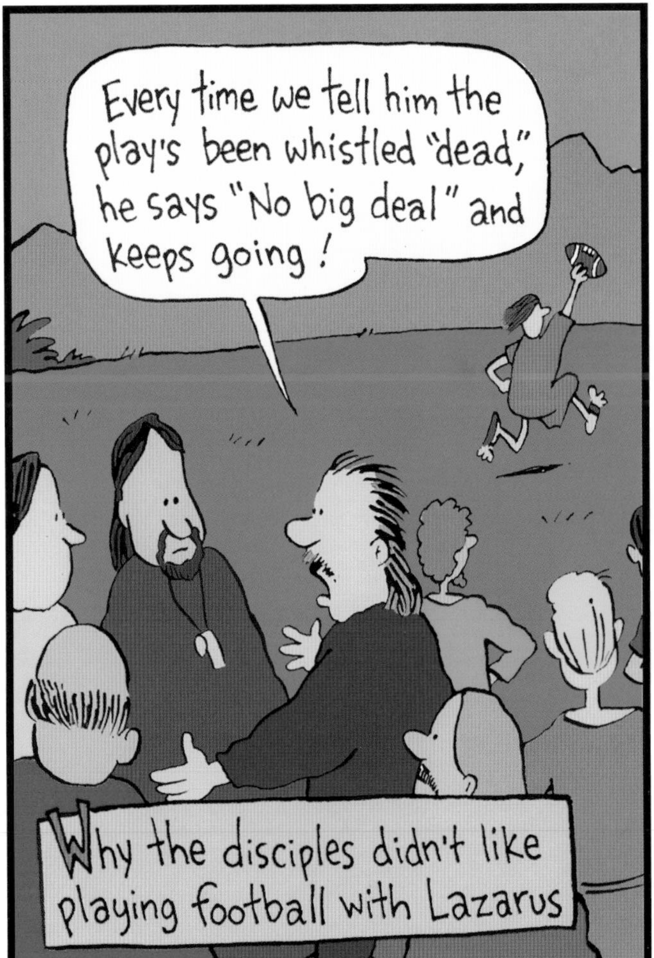
Every time we tell him the play's been whistled "dead," he says "No big deal" and keeps going!
Why the disciples didn't like playing football with Lazarus

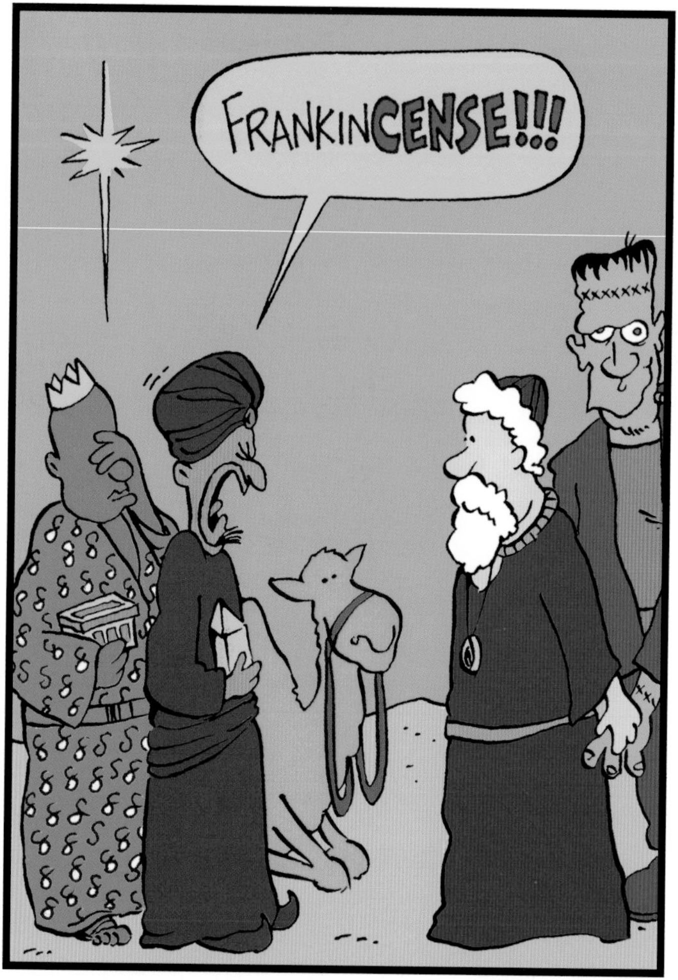
FRANKINCENSE!!!

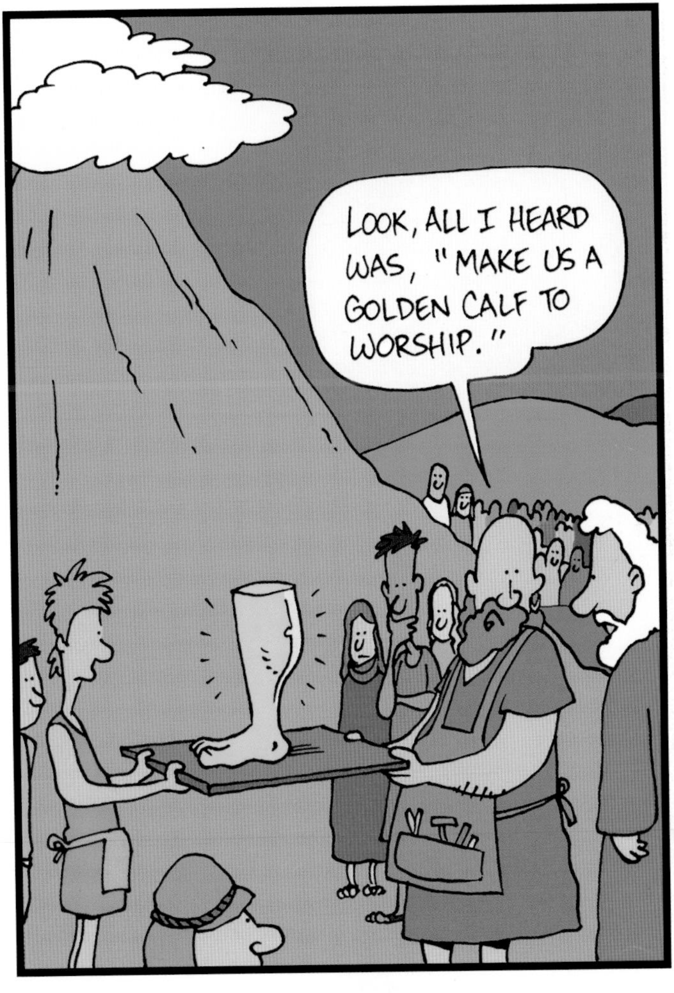
LOOK, ALL I HEARD WAS, "MAKE US A GOLDEN CALF TO WORSHIP."

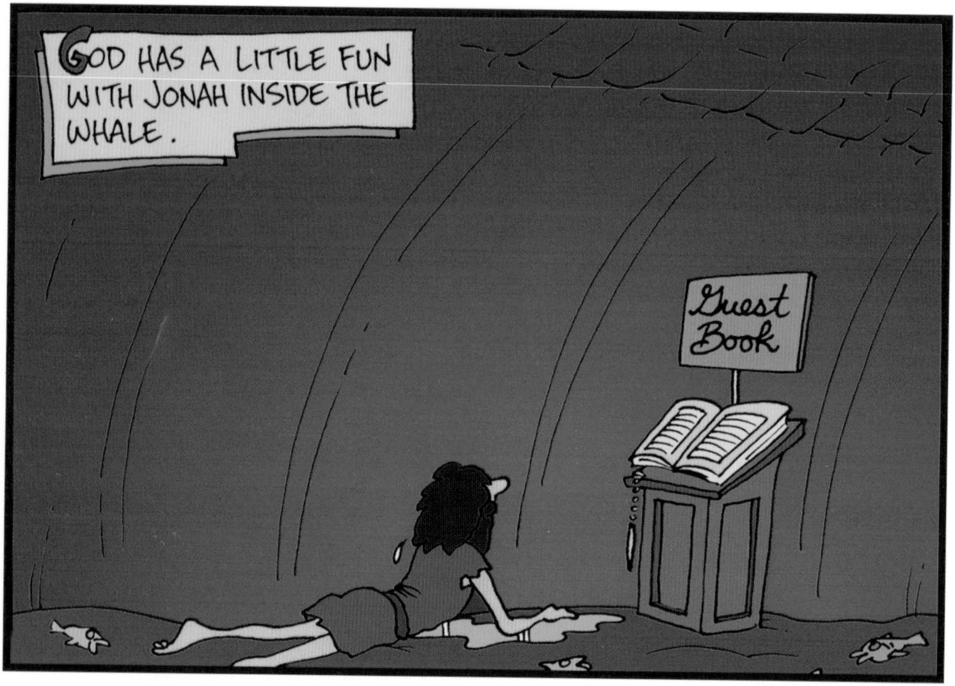
GOD HAS A LITTLE FUN WITH JONAH INSIDE THE WHALE.
Guest Book

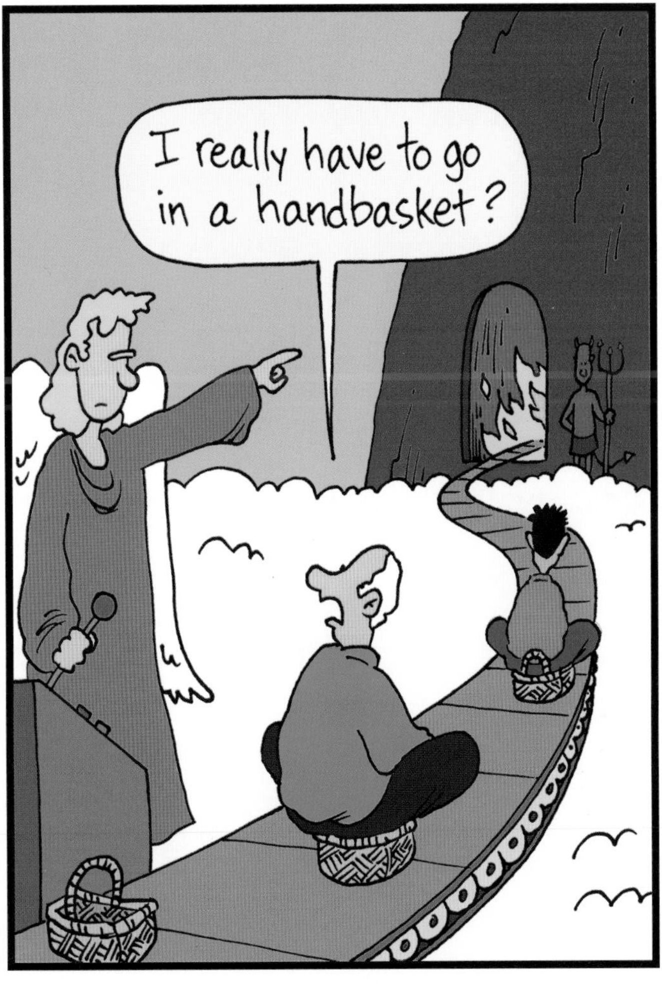
I really have to go in a handbasket?

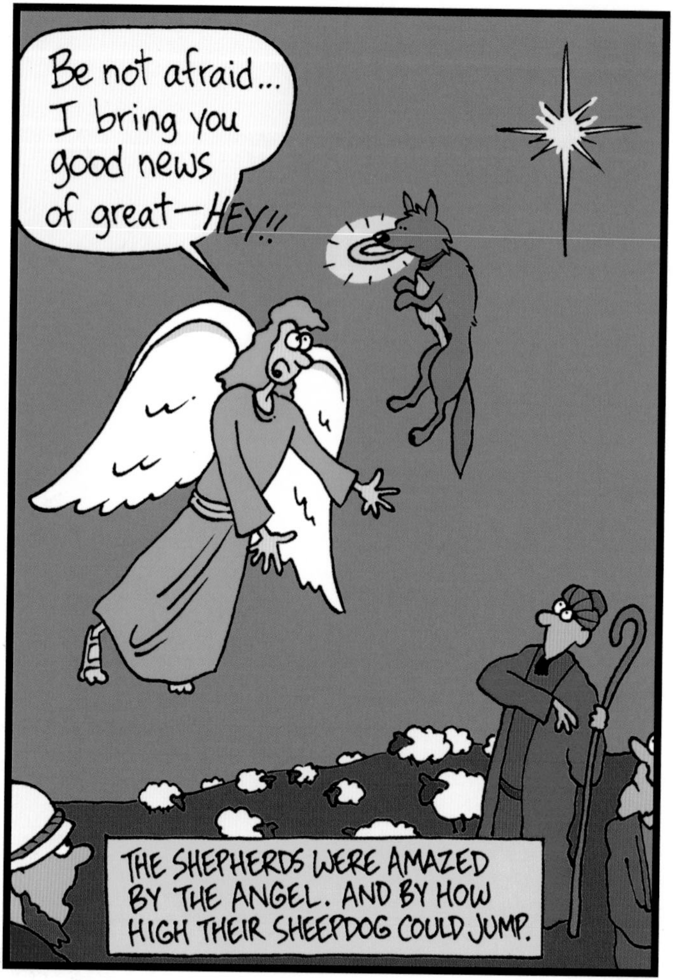
Be not afraid... I bring you good news of great—HEY!!
THE SHEPHERDS WERE AMAZED BY THE ANGEL. AND BY HOW HIGH THEIR SHEEPDOG COULD JUMP.

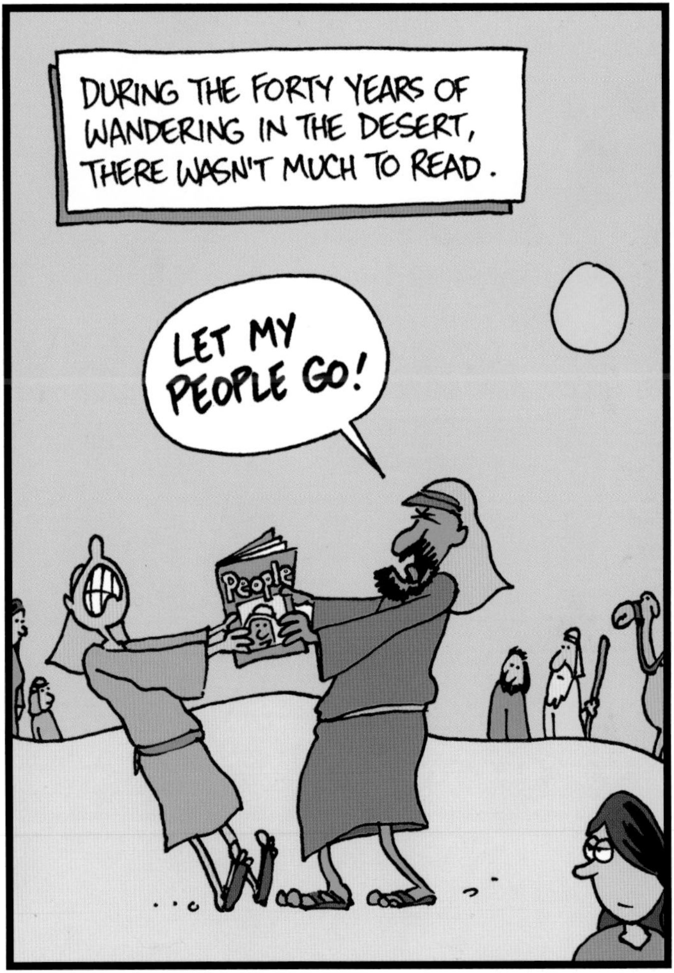
DURING THE FORTY YEARS OF WANDERING IN THE DESERT, THERE WASN'T MUCH TO READ.
LET MY PEOPLE GO!
People

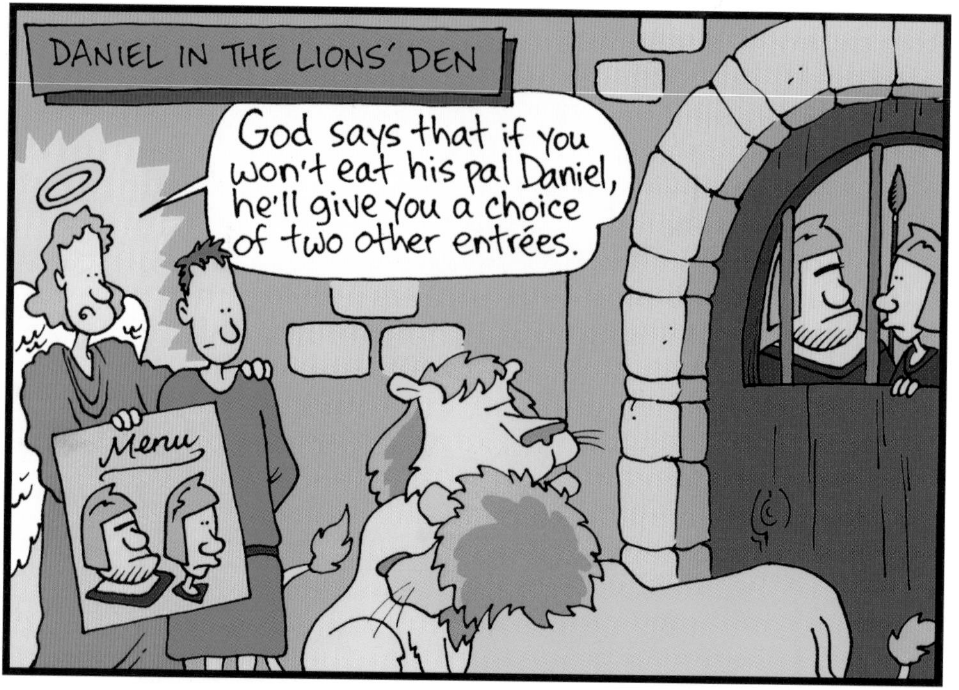
DANIEL IN THE LIONS' DEN
God says that if you won't eat his pal Daniel, he'll give you a choice of two other entrées.
Menu

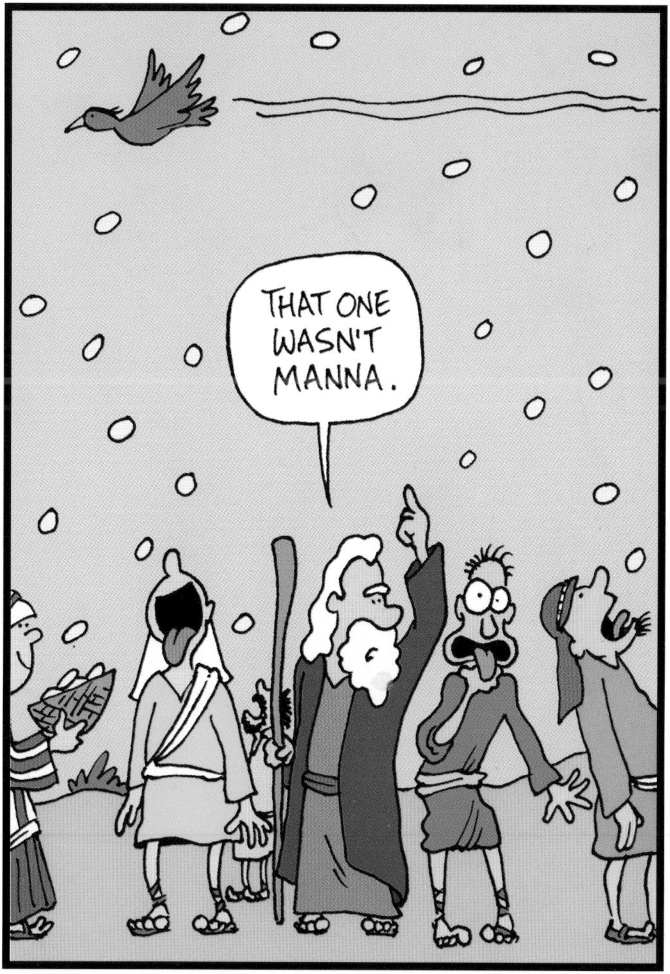
THAT ONE WASN'T MANNA.

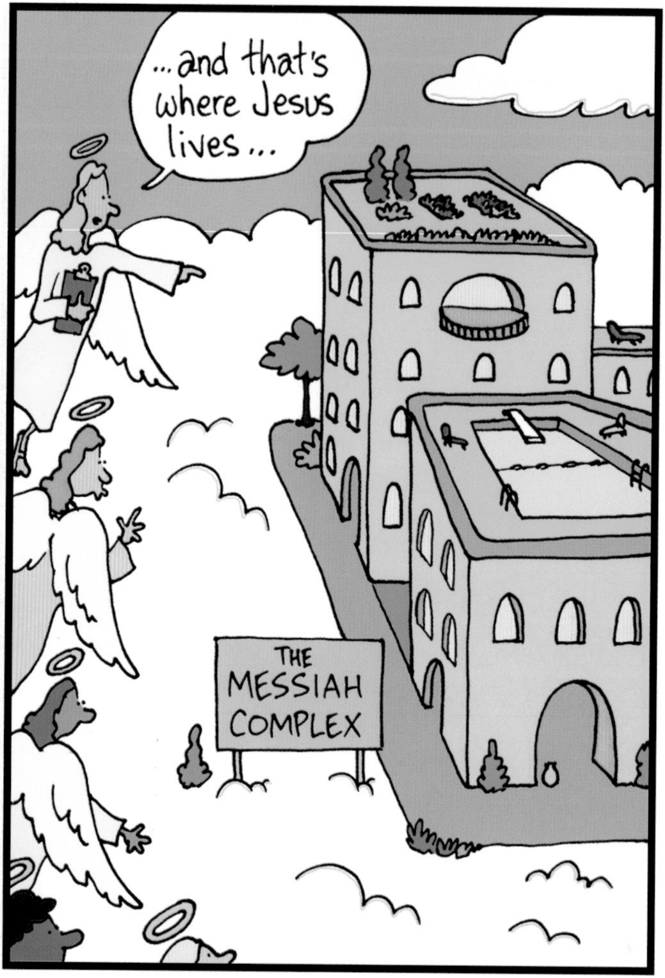
...and that's where Jesus lives...
THE MESSIAH COMPLEX

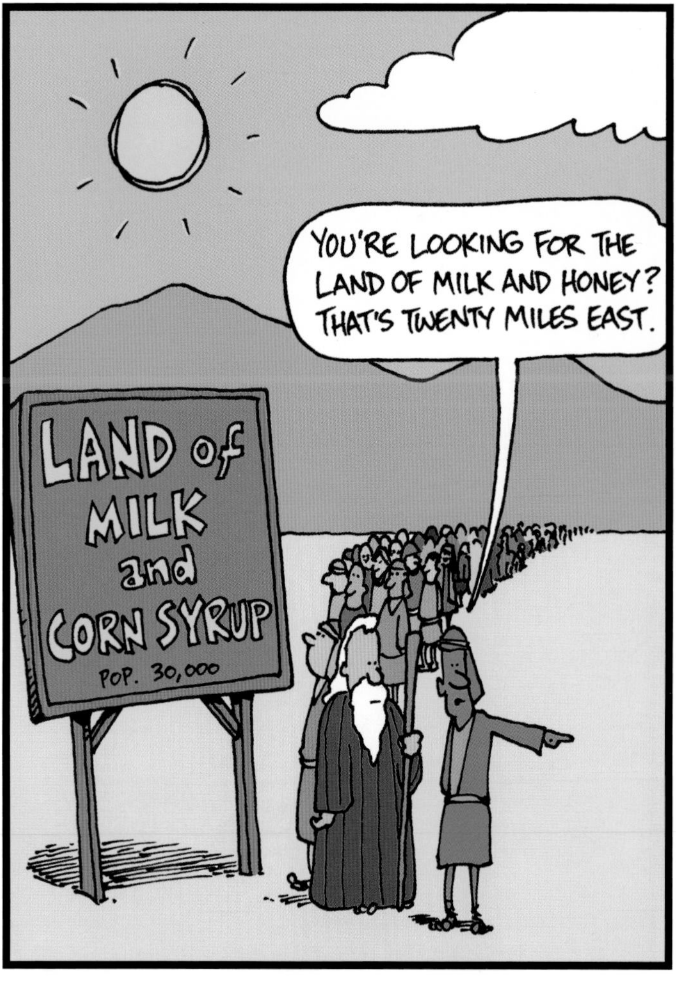
YOU'RE LOOKING FOR THE LAND OF MILK AND HONEY? THAT'S TWENTY MILES EAST.
LAND of MILK and CORN SYRUP
POP. 30,000

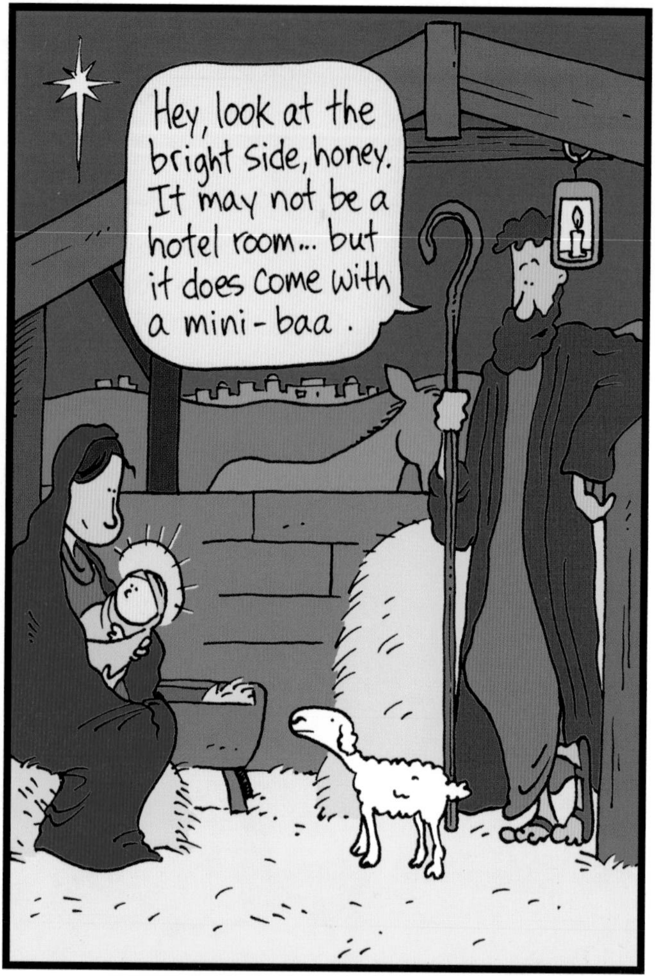
Hey, look at the bright side, honey. It may not be a hotel room... but it does come with a mini-baa.

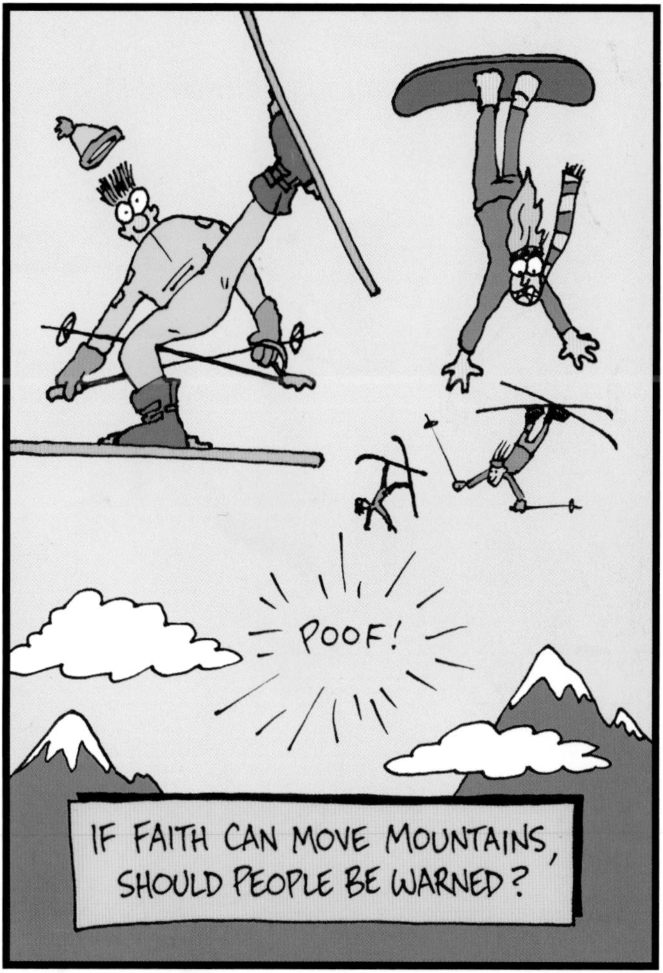
POOF!
IF FAITH CAN MOVE MOUNTAINS, SHOULD PEOPLE BE WARNED?

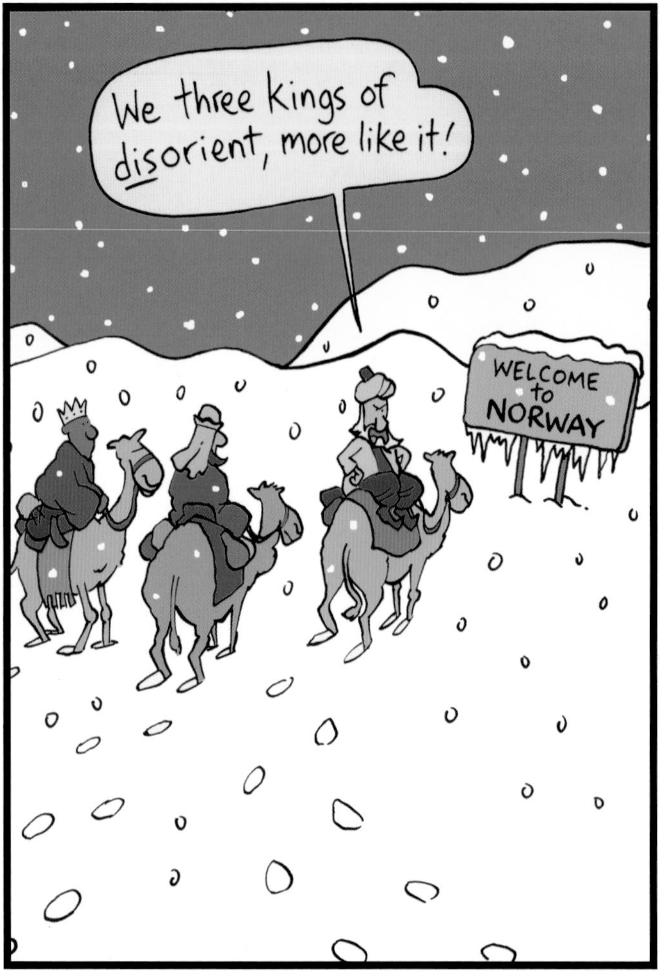
We three kings of disorient, more like it!
WELCOME to NORWAY

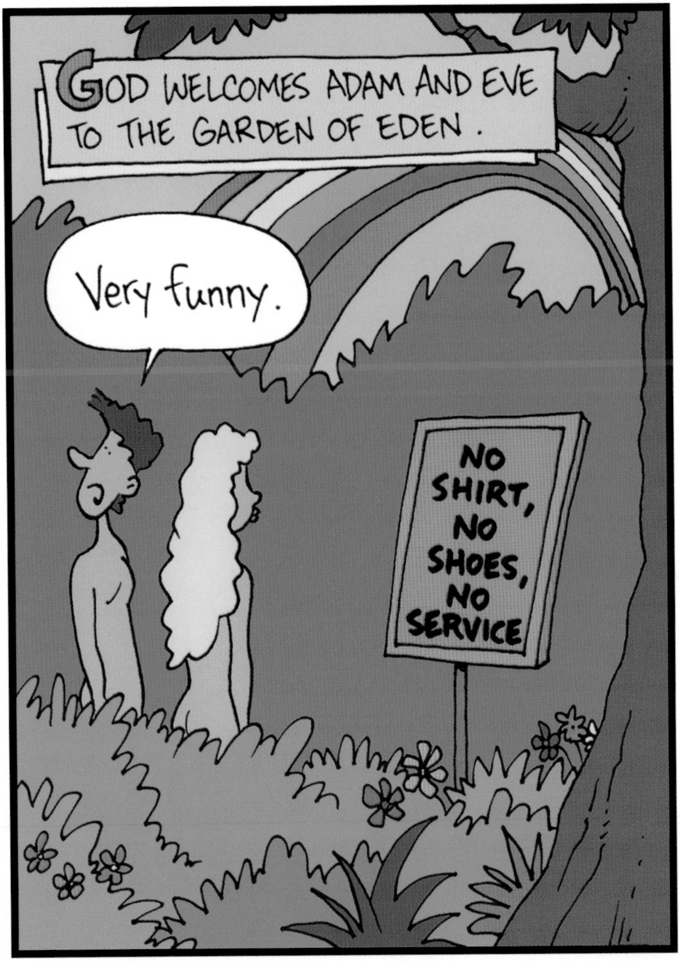
GOD WELCOMES ADAM AND EVE TO THE GARDEN OF EDEN.
Very funny.
NO SHIRT, NO SHOES, NO SERVICE

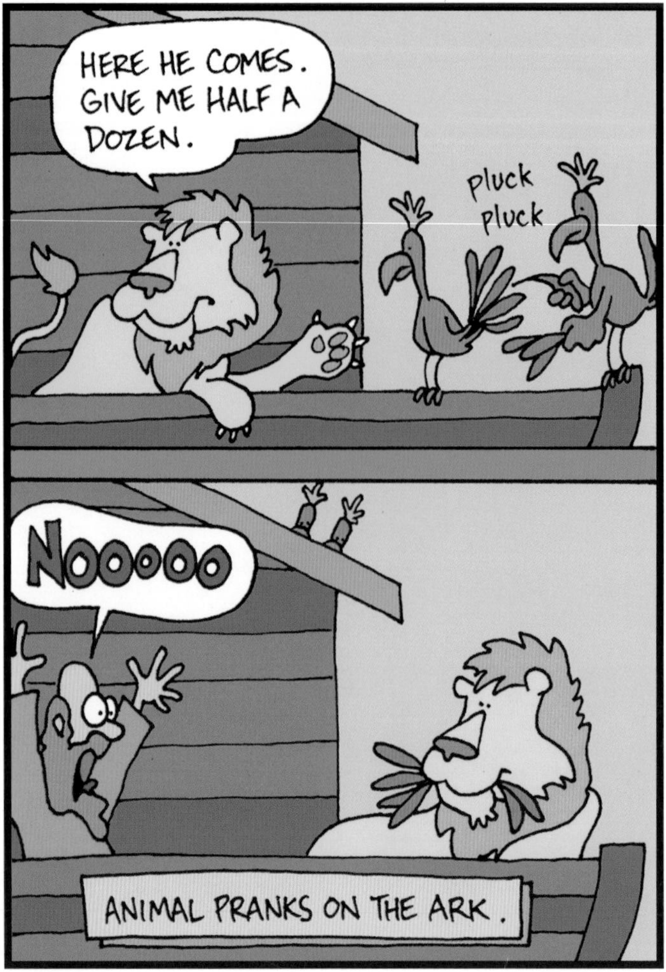
HERE HE COMES. GIVE ME HALF A DOZEN.
pluck pluck
NOOOOO
ANIMAL PRANKS ON THE ARK.

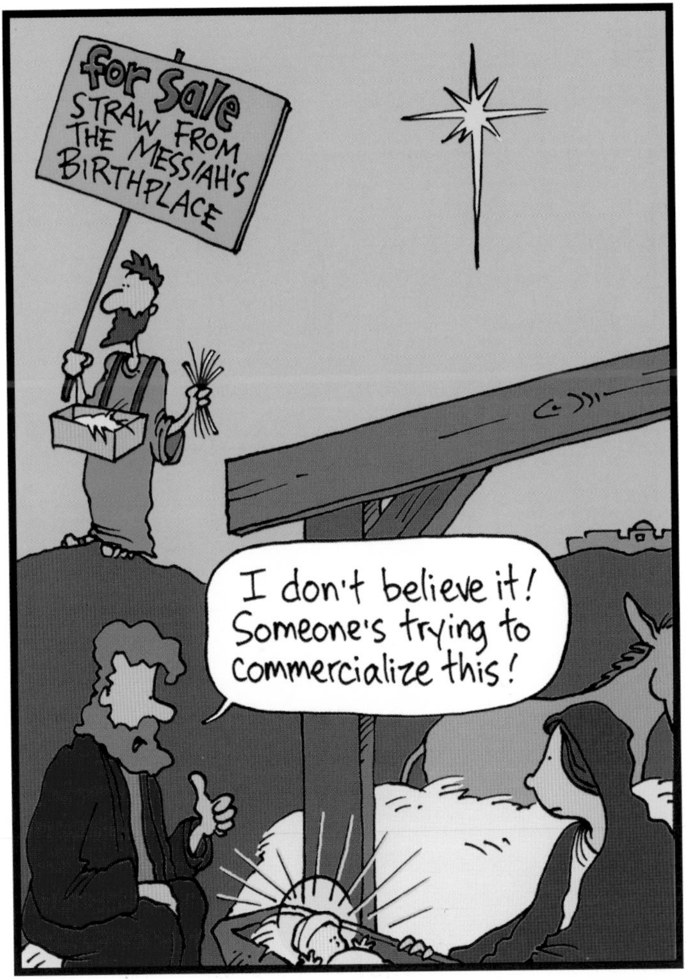
for Sale
STRAW FROM THE MESSIAH'S BIRTHPLACE
I don't believe it! Someone's trying to commercialize this!

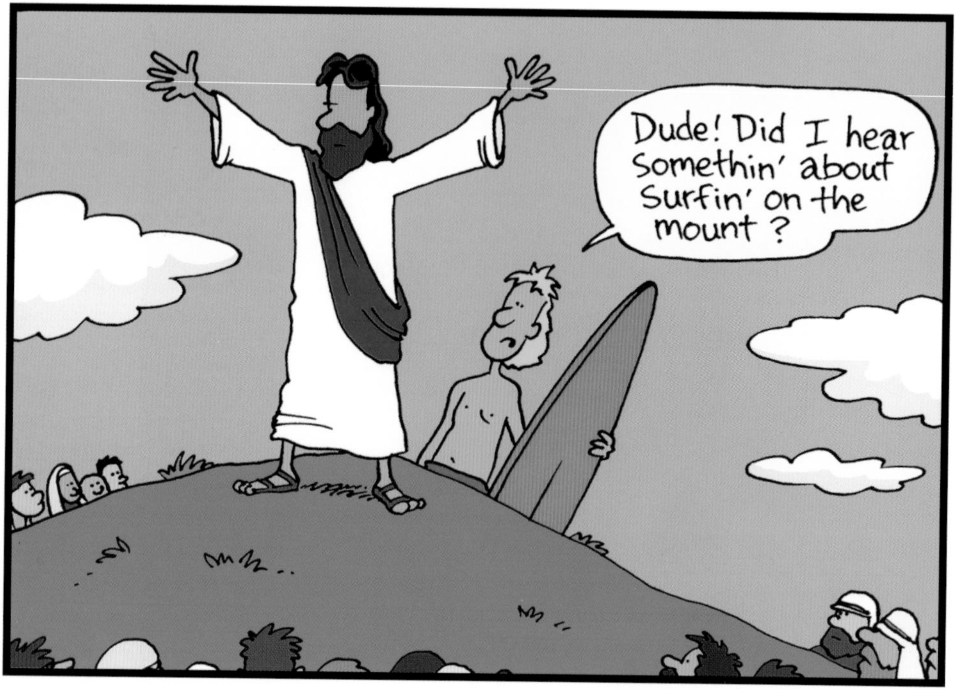
Dude! Did I hear Somethin' about Surfin' on the mount?

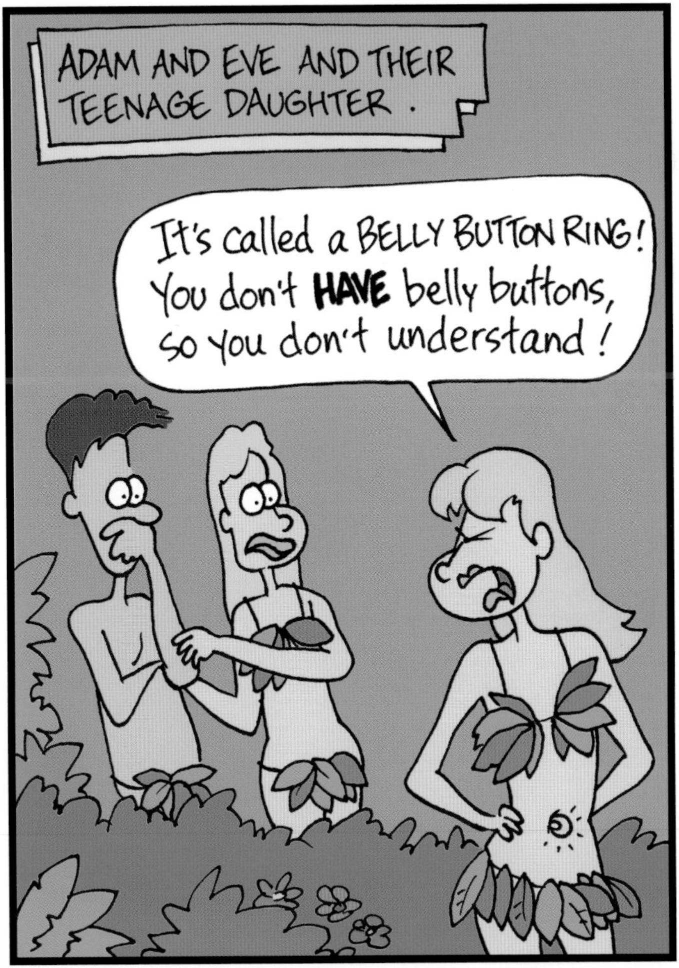
ADAM AND EVE AND THEIR TEENAGE DAUGHTER.
It's called a BELLY BUTTON RING! You don't **HAVE** belly buttons, so you don't understand!

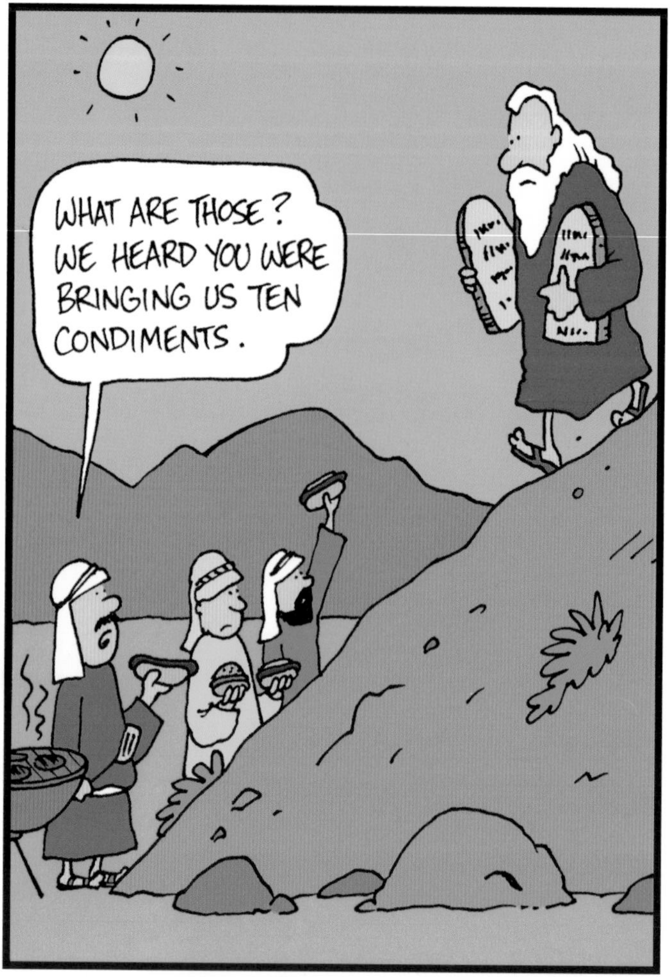
WHAT ARE THOSE? WE HEARD YOU WERE BRINGING US TEN CONDIMENTS.

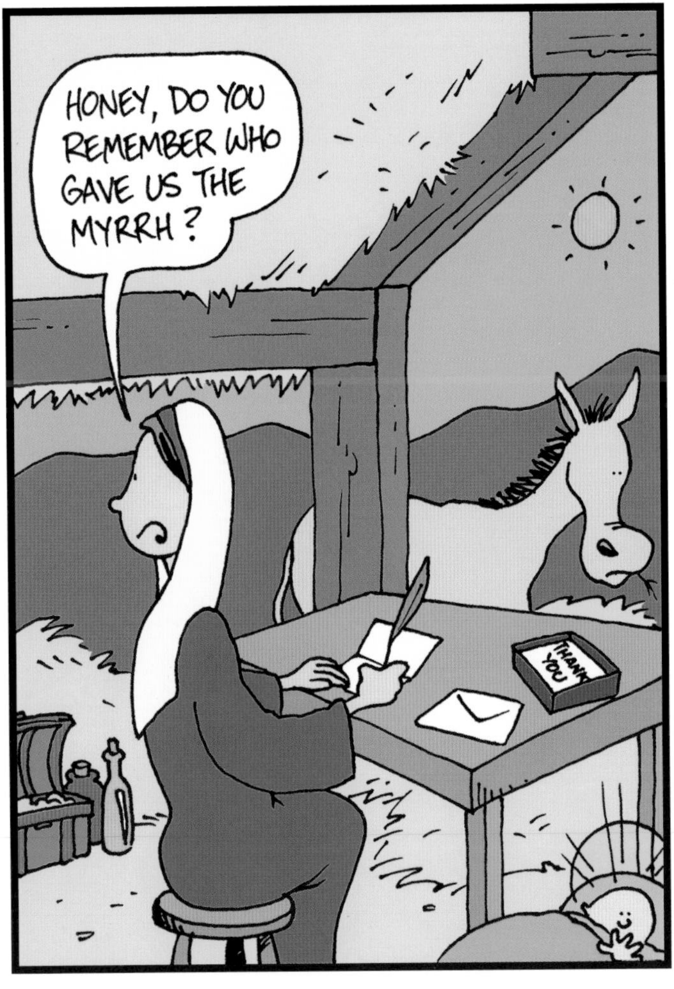
HONEY, DO YOU REMEMBER WHO GAVE US THE MYRRH?
THANK YOU

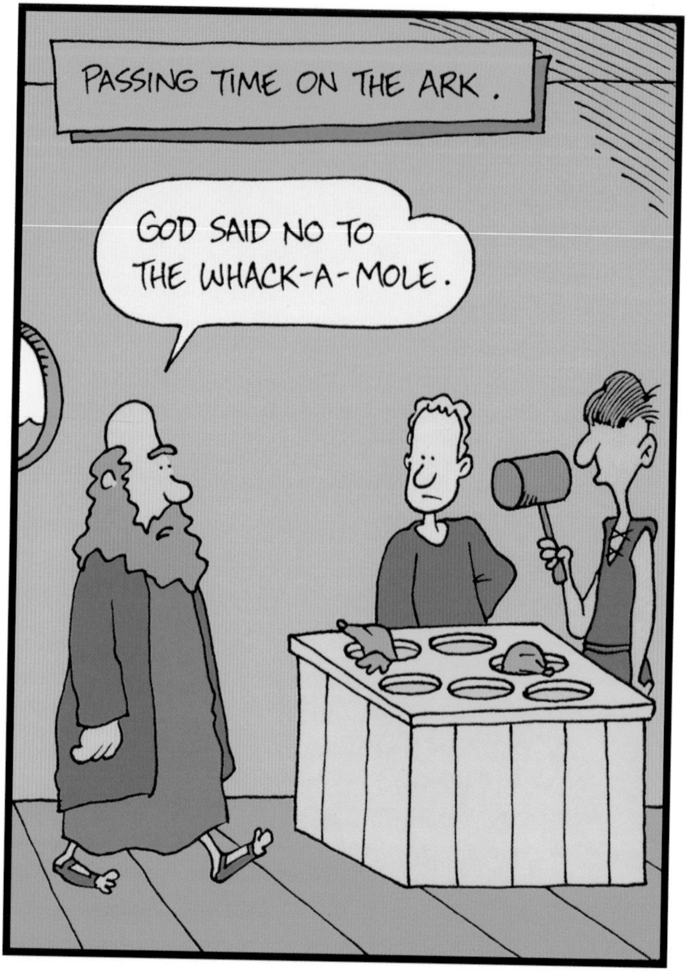
PASSING TIME ON THE ARK.
GOD SAID NO TO THE WHACK-A-MOLE.

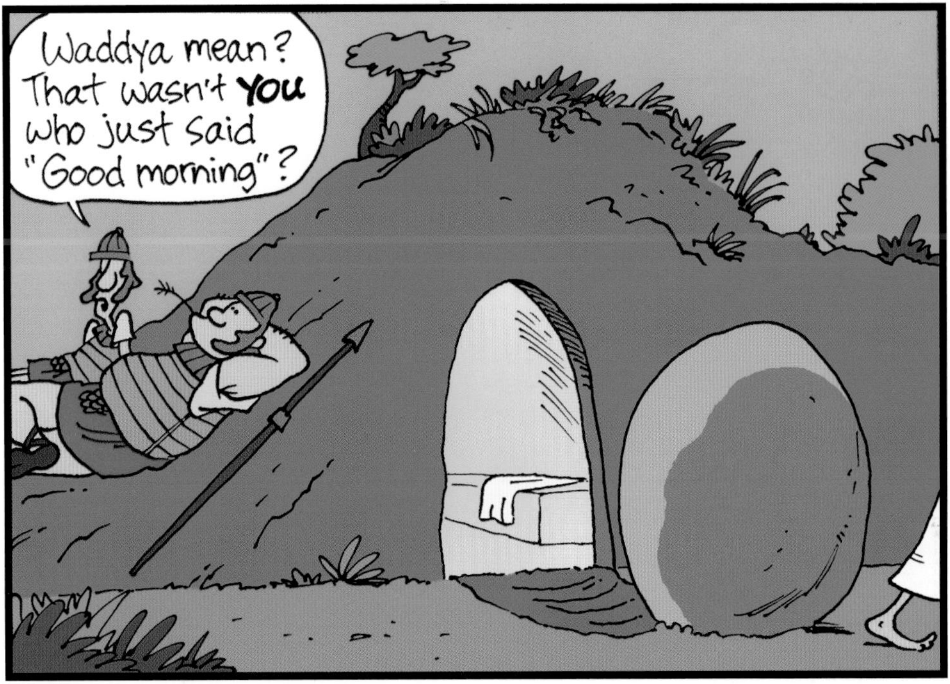
Waddya mean? That wasn't YOU who just said "Good morning"?

THERE'S A WORLD OF LAUGHTER

FOR YOU TO EXPLORE AT

inheritthemirth.com

GREETING CARDS!

CALENDARS!

POSTERS!

MAGNETS!

POSTCARDS!

AND MORE!

God has brought me laughter.

Genesis 21:6

At Inspirio, we'd love to hear your
stories and your feedback.
Please send your comments to us
by way of email at
icares@zondervan.com
or to the address below:

inspirio

Attn: Inspirio Cares
5300 Patterson Avenue SE
Grand Rapids, MI 49530

If you would like further information
about Inspirio and the products we create,
please visit us at:
www.inspiriogifts.com

Thank you and God bless!